CONTENTS

Tables and figures	vii
Acknowledgements	xi
Abbreviations	xiii
Series Editor's Preface	xv
Chapter 1. The Global Village and the Ivory Tower	1
The context of inquiry	4
Entering the global newsroom	8
On television	11
Coming up next	12
Chapter 2. Colliding Worlds	17
Critical theoretical perspectives	18
'Big business equals bad journalism as corporations control info flow'	21
Contra-flows and counter-hegemonic media	22
The story of Russia Today	26
The story of Al Jazeera English	28
Worlds apart?	32

Chapter 3. A World in Crisis: Atlas Reports 37
Global crises in global news headlines 38
Reporting the Arab uprisings 45
CNNI and the Arab uprisings 46
BBC World and the Arab uprisings 49
RT and the Arab uprisings 50
AJE and the Arab uprisings 50
Bearing witness 52
To wrap up 57

Chapter 4. Brave New World 61
The problem of representation 64
Space, place and news maps 66
The space of Europe 69
The space of Europe in BBCW 72
The space of Europe in AJE 73
The space of Europe in RT 74
Just stories 76
Wasted lives 76
The course of rehabilitation 78
Rodeo rehab 79
Cosmopolitan geographies 80

Chapter 5. Another World: Europe as Other 85
Seeing Europe through other eyes (orientation) 90
It was a lot of fun but very strange (discussion/evaluation/resolution) 104
Europe is progress, Africa is respect (coda) 106

Chapter 6. A World of Difference 109
To sum up, here is the main news in brief 110
Between crisis.... 114
...and cosmopolitanism 115
The view from the ivory tower and on the ground (theory and practice) 116
Returning to the global village 119

Notes 123
References 127
Index 149

ALEXA ROBERTSON

GLOBAL NEWS

REPORTING CONFLICTS AND COSMOPOLITANISM

PETER LANG
New York • Bern • Frankfurt • Berlin
Brussels • Vienna • Oxford • Warsaw

Library of Congress Cataloging-in-Publication Data

Robertson, Alexa.
Global news: reporting conflicts and cosmopolitanism / Alexa Robertson.
pages cm. — (Global crises and the media; 17)
Includes bibliographical references and index.
1. Violence—Press coverage. 2. Social conflict—Press coverage.
3. War—Press coverage. 4. Journalism—Objectivity. 5. Cosmopolitanism.
6. Mass media and globalization. I. Title.
PN4784.V56R63 303.6—dc23 2014043813
ISBN 978-1-4331-2425-9 (hardcover)
ISBN 978-1-4331-2424-2 (paperback)
ISBN 978-1-4539-1503-5 (e-book)
ISSN 1947-2587

Bibliographic information published by **Die Deutsche Nationalbibliothek**.
Die Deutsche Nationalbibliothek lists this publication in the "Deutsche Nationalbibliografie"; detailed bibliographic data are available on the Internet at http://dnb.d-nb.de/.

Cover image: *The Tower of Babel* (*Turmbau zu Babel*) by Pieter Bruegel d.Ä.
Reproduced courtesy of the Kunsthistorisches Museum, Vienna

The paper in this book meets the guidelines for permanence and durability of the Committee on Production Guidelines for Book Longevity of the Council of Library Resources.

29 Broadway, 18th floor, New York, NY 10006
www.peterlang.com

Printed in the United States of America

TABLES AND FIGURES

Figure 3.1. Number of different countries occurring in headlines of Al Jazeera English, BBC World, CNN International and Russia Today, January 2011 & January 2013 combined (233 broadcasts coded) and the number of countries occurring in 'crisis' headlines (figures in parentheses).

Table 3.1. Headlines in Al Jazeera English, BBC World, CNN International and Russia Today, January 2011 & January 2013 combined (233 broadcasts coded), distributed according to whether they are the sort of crisis referred to by Cottle (2009, 'Cottle heads'), other sorts of crisis (violent or violently repressed protests, political crises, other), and whether they can be considered 'global' ("encompass or move across geographical terrains and political territories").

Table 3.2. Crises headlines in Al Jazeera English, BBC World, CNN International and Russia Today, January 2011 & January 2013 combined (233 broadcasts coded) distributed according to crisis category.

Table 3.3. Distribution of material in the analysis of 'Arab uprising' reporting

Table 3.4. Distribution of sources (people with speaking parts, counted once for every news item they speak in) in reports concerning the Arab uprisings on BBC World 9 pm CET and Al Jazeera English 8 pm CET, Monday 10 January–Sunday 30 January 2011.

Table 3.5. Number of items on the Arab uprisings filed by a reporter (and not just read by the anchor) in BBC World 9 pm CET and Al Jazeera English 8 pm CET, Monday 10 January–Sunday 30 January 2011, distinguished by gender and whether they are on site.

Table 4.1. Hierarchy of issues in reports of Europe, 1 minute or more in length, broadcast on BBC World News, Al Jazeera English and Russia Today, 1 May–11 June 2014.

Table 4.2. The space of Europe: countries comprising Europe, and the nationalities of people speaking in reports of Europe, 1 minute or more in length, broadcast on BBC World News, Al Jazeera English and Russia Today, 1 May-11 June 2014.

Plate 5.1. The Europe of the imagination. A musician in African sings about people dreaming of adventures in Europe, in the first episode of the *Surprising Europe* series, *Taking the Leap*, http://www.aljazeera.com/programmes/surprisingeurope/2011/08/20118695843266691.html. Image reproduced with permission from Witfilm, http://witfilm.nl.

Plate 5.2. The Europe of directly lived experience. Michael, from Ghana, talks about the hardships of surviving in Spain in the second episode of the *Surprising Europe* series, *Hopes and Dreams*, http://www.aljazeera.com/programmes/surprisingeurope/2011/08/201186102630499582.html. Image reproduced with permission from Witfilm, http://witfilm.nl.

Plate 5.3. Living like animals. Ssuuna, from Uganda, visits a dog hotel in the Netherlands and discovers how well they live, in contrast to undocumented migrants in Europe, in the third episode of the *Surprising Europe* series, *Making Ends Meet*, http://www.aljazeera.com/programmes/surprisingeurope/2011/08/20118168557626755.html. Image reproduced with permission from Witfilm, http://witfilm.nl.

Plate 5.4. Europe as a strange place. Baba, from Ghana, reports from the Spanish town of Bunol, where 250 thousand kilograms of tomatoes are destroyed in a few hours of revelry, in the fourth episode of the *Surprising Europe* series, *Under Pressure*, http://www.aljazeera.com/programmes/surprisingeurope/2011/08/201183065919297868.html. Image reproduced with permission from Witfilm, http://witfilm.nl.

Plate 5.5. Europe as difficult to understand. Ssuuna, from Uganda, watches as Dutch bathers plunge into an icy sea on New Year's Day, in the fifth episode of the *Surprising Europe* series, *Culture Shock*, http://www.aljazeera.com/programmes/surprisingeurope/. Image reproduced with permission from Witfilm, http://witfilm.nl.

Plate 5.6. Unbelievable Europe. An innocent migrant is kept at the detention centre in Zeist in the sixth episode of the *Surprising Europe* series, *Running Out of Luck*, http://www.aljazeera.com/programmes/surprisingeurope/. Image reproduced with permission from Witfilm, http://witfilm.nl.

Plate 5.7. Lonely Europe. Ssuuna visits an old folks' home in the Netherlands, where the elderly live instead of with their children and grandchildren, in the eighth episode of the *Surprising Europe* series, *The Good Life*, http://www.aljazeera.com/programmes/surprisingeurope/. Image reproduced with permission from Witfilm, http://witfilm.nl.

Plate 5.8. Africa Surprising Europe. Italian-born Annie, who longs to 'return' to Liberia, stands in the centre of Rome and sings 'This is Africa, surprising Europe' in the ninth and final episode of the *Surprising Europe* series, *Home Sweet Home*, http://www.aljazeera.com/programmes/surprisingeurope/2011/10/20111049374961442.html. Image reproduced with permission from Witfilm, http://witfilm.nl.

ACKNOWLEDGEMENTS

First things first: the research reported in this book was made possible thanks to funding by the Swedish Research Council (grant number 421–2009–1698/90169801).

I am grateful to the journalists and news executives at AJE Doha, London and Washington and at RT in Moscow who took the time to explain their work and open the doors to their workplaces. I am indebted to Kristina Riegert for conducting the Doha interviews, to Tine Figenschou for advice about how to go about doing so, and to Clarie Åkesson for helping to transcribe them. Paul Levin transcribed the RT interview that features in Chapter 2, and was an enthusiastic discussion partner in the planning stages of the empirical study.

A special vote of thanks to Leone Serrander, with whom I have spent many an hour shoulder-to-shoulder, coding endless news broadcasts, and who helped with the research that went into the first set of empirical analyses reported in Chapter 3. Working with Leone made drudgery rather fun, and the quality and reliability of the results were improved by her diligence. I sometimes wonder whether she was sent to me by the patron saint of university lecturers who try to combine teaching and research (whom I suspect is Saint Jude, the patron saint of lost causes). I am also grateful for the work of Erik Jönsson who, upon being asked whether he really knew what he was getting into (given that coding hundreds of news reports can do strange things to your head) replied reassuringly and insightfully that a World of Warcraft guildmaster has the requisite stamina.

Alexandra Segerberg was extremely helpful—as she always is—when talking and thinking through the structure, and indeed point, of the book. Eva-Karin Olsson, Ester Pollack and Gunilla Hultén offered useful thoughts on early versions of the empirical analyses of crisis reporting, for which I am grateful. Thanks also to the Masters students at the Department of Media Studies at Stockholm University (IMS) who have taken my course on Global Media Studies over the years. The insights and enthusiasm of these students—and the thought of engaging with their successors—has given me the impetus to write the book. I would also like to thank Simon Cottle and Mary Savigar for supporting the publication and giving constructive guidance. The anonymous reviewers who gave feedback on the design and contents of the book shaped the final outcome in significant ways.

There is an abundance of news material within easy reach of those interested in studying and writing about it. For the scholar intent on conducting systematic, comparative analysis of television coverage over time, however, there is decidedly less on offer. Three people helped ensure that all was not lost. I am very grateful to Christine Ericsdotter and Henrik Nordgren at the Stockholm University language lab for cheerfully giving my media library a berth, thus making it possible to access valuable research material at a reasonable cost. But most of all, I would like to thank Bernard Devine, without whose technological ingenuity I could not do the sort of research and teaching that I do. During the decade or more that we have been looking for solutions to primary-source-material problems, he has been vigilant, creative and quite simply a deus ex 'Mac'ina. I dedicate this book to him, with heartfelt thanks.

ABBREVIATIONS

AJE	Al Jazeera English
BBCW	BBC World
CNNI	CNN International
EU	European Union
RT	Russia Today
UNESCO	United Nations Educational, Scientific and Cultural Organization

SERIES EDITOR'S PREFACE

Global Crises and the Media

We live in a global age. We inhabit a world that has become radically interconnected, interdependent, and communicated in the formations and flows of the media. This same world also spawns proliferating, often interpenetrating, "global crises."

From climate change to the war on terror, financial meltdowns to forced migrations, energy shortages to world poverty, and humanitarian disasters to the denial of human rights, these and other crises represent the dark side of our globalized planet. Their origins and outcomes are not confined behind national borders and they are not best conceived through national prisms of understanding. The impacts of global crises often register across "sovereign" national territories, surrounding regions and beyond, and they can also become subject to systems of governance and forms of civil society response that are no less encompassing or transnational in scope. In today's interdependent world, global crises cannot be regarded as exceptional or aberrant events only, erupting without rhyme or reason or dislocated from the contemporary world (dis)order. They are endemic to the contemporary global world, deeply enmeshed within it. And so too are they highly dependent on the world's media and communication networks.

The series *Global Crises and the Media* sets out to examine not only the media's role in the *communication* of global threats and crises but also how they can variously enter into their *constitution*, enacting them on the public stage and helping to shape their future trajectory around the world. More specifically, the volumes in this series seek to: (1) contextualize the study of global crisis reporting and representations in relation to wider debates about the changing flows and formations of world media communication; (2) address how global crises become variously communicated and contested in both so-called "old" and "new" media around the world; (3) consider the possible impacts of global crisis reporting on public awareness, political action, and policy responses; (4) showcase the very latest research findings and discussion from leading authorities in their respective fields of inquiry; and (5) contribute to the development of positions of theory and debate that deliberately move beyond national parochialisms and/or geographically disaggregated research agendas. In these ways the specially commissioned books in the *Global Crises and the Media* series aim to provide a sophisticated and empirically engaged understanding of the media's changing roles in global crises and thereby contribute to academic and public debate about some of the most significant global threats, conflicts, and contentions in the world today.

Global News: Reporting Conflicts and Cosmopolitanism by Alexa Robertson perfectly fits the series remit above. Her disquisition on the contemporary complexities and contingencies of world news reporting offers an incisive and up-to-the-moment engagement with the changing nature of television broadcasting around the world. Importantly, and unusually, it approaches its subject matter through twin optics. One is informed by and authoritatively versed in preceding positions of theory focused on the play of vested interests and ideologies. The latter have frequently been academically observed and critically interrogated in the reporting of major conflicts by world broadcasters who, notwithstanding their universalizing claims to the contrary, too often toe the national line, peddle comforting elite myths and seemingly dance to the political economy tune. A differing optic, that of emergent cosmopolitanism, invites us to consider both the current practices and promise of today's journalism through a more benevolently inflected lens. Here world news is approached not simply or only as the vehicle for vested material interests and venal powerplays, but also a medium that can sometimes display and discharge a seemingly more humanitarian, human rights and human security conscious responsibility to others around the globe. Sometimes this is performed and enacted in and through the cultural recognition afforded to former 'Others', valorizing cultural differences and respecting different cultural practices. Sometimes we witness it in the professional journalists' elicitations to their audiences to care as they do and to therefore empathize and demonstrate concern. This is discharged in and through skillfully crafted film reports or inscribed in other ways into their journalistic reports of major conflicts and humanitarian disasters. Robertson's book eloquently and productively moves within and across these twin optics, powerfully adjudicating between differing theoretical and political claims within the field of world news study. The analysis and discussion is all the more robust for being based on a solid platform of data and close empirical analysis of some of the key world broadcasters and their recent news reporting. This is a timely study and one that not only chimes with the Global Crisis and Media Series but also current debates and the emergent complexities of contemporary news study. As Series Editor I am pleased to recommend it to you.

Simon Cottle, Series Editor

· 1 ·

THE GLOBAL VILLAGE AND THE IVORY TOWER

This book is about the different worlds of global television news—theoretical, empirical and imaginative. In the theoretical realm, global news has been understood in terms of capitalist profit, political propaganda, technological empowerment, cultural connectivity and morality. On an empirical level, the institutional and political contexts in which global newsrooms flourish or founder are worlds apart. Those which feature in these pages are funded by classic democracies, an authoritarian state, and a family dynasty, and each is moored in a different part of the globe, representative, it could be argued, of both 'the West' and 'the Rest' (to paraphrase Stuart Hall). In the realm of the imagination, the newsworlds available to global audiences differ in intriguing ways as well, and one of this study's main contributions to scholarship on media globalization is to show how they do. While the impact of such differences can only be established by studying global audience reception—a task which lies beyond the scope of this book, just as the funding for such an endeavour lies far beyond the grasp of most hermeneutically minded social scientists—the comparative analysis of global newsrooms' depictions of the world is a start. It provides a point of entry into what Keane (2003: 169) described as 'narrated, imagined, non-violent spaces' in which power can be scrutinized, praised and condemned by millions of people throughout the world 'in defiance of the old tyrannies of space and time'.

Those tyrannies have been under siege for a while. Half a century ago, McLuhan argued that the Western world was 'imploding' (McLuhan & Gordon 2013/1964). Technological advances in the age of machines had made it possible for people to extend their bodies in space, but subsequent advances in media technology during the 'electrical age' went further. Humanity had the resources to extend its central nervous system 'in a global embrace', McLuhan famously wrote, 'abolishing both space and time'. His prescient text of 1964 looked ahead to a near future 'when the creative process of knowing will be collectively and corporately extended to the whole of human society' as a result of sense-widening by the media (McLuhan & Gordon 2013/1964: 5). In a world shaped by media flows, he saw people becoming involved in the whole of humanity: 'the globe is no more than a village'. To McLuhan, this meant that playing an aloof, dissociated part was no longer an option. Years later, in the digital age, Beck (2006) would make the same claim, albeit using different words, pronouncing that people were becoming cosmopolitans 'by default'.

McLuhan engaged in the liberal use of metaphors to describe how developments in media technology impacted society. This book uses metaphors too—of different worlds—each meant to describe the vantage point taken on the global media landscape by scholars looking out of the ivory tower through a different window. Like other windows and frames, metaphors can narrow the vision, reducing often sophisticated arguments to a few words. They can also guide and, at best, expand our thinking, however. Some of McLuhan's metaphors have weathered the passage of time, and the global village is perhaps that which has proven most enduring, one piece of empirical evidence being the fact that a Google search on the term generates over 90 million hits.

The metaphorical image of the ivory tower (not attributable to McLuhan) is arguably less relevant to contemporary academia, but I want to use it because of the impression formed, through reading over the years, that scholars of global communication can at times seem curiously divorced from the 'real' world of newsmaking, as if they look down on the media landscape from the lofty height of the tower, from which vantage point the ecology takes on abstract form or (from the perspective of another window) appears as a terrain of capital rather than information flows. It elides in my imagination with Pieter Bruegel the Elder's painting of the Tower of Babel, partly because that masterpiece is often used as an illustration of the intellectual space inhabited by researchers, and partly because it seems that the participants in the academic discussion of global communication tend to speak quite different scholarly languages. While it is often said that we must move beyond analyses of content, empirical engagement with global media output—the stories told by journalists to their viewers across the world, and the meanings enfolded in these stories—remains a finite resource. Systematic comparative analysis of global television content, in particular, is conspicuous by its absence. The metaphor of the ivory tower is thus deployed here provocatively, to represent this distance from the real work of the global newsroom, which is not a metaphor in this book, but rather the object of study. At the same time, the reader is invited to envisage Breugel's tower with a satellite dish on top, because those who work in it are of course immersed in the global media flows they study.

What all participants in the discussion have in their sights is a communicative space that is not necessarily beyond, but which is perhaps best thought of as straddling national borders. Different metaphors to describe this space have been used by different authors. Some have sought to transpose the Habermasian exchange of information and debate from the coffee house and the national setting to that of a 'global public sphere'. These attempts have generally been less successful than McLuhan's, for his metaphor makes no attempt to include the moral, the political or the pedagogical, or to engage with the problem of where to put the state. Solutions to that conundrum range from shoving it into a conceptual closet with the clutter of concepts one can't bring oneself to discard, but which used to work a lot better (such as 'foreign news'), to sweeping it out to make way for the fittings of a brave new world, as did Silverstone (2007) with his concept of mediapolis (an image of a hopeful, moral space created by the media under globalization). Tomlinson (2011) and Stevenson (2003; 1999) are among those who have looked thoughtfully into this moral, pedagogical room, with a connecting door on 'reality' furnished by the media, and sized it up. Scholars like these, who see a cosmopolitan and not just conflictual world reflected in media output, are interested in the communicative place where we are no longer aloof—where we make the acquaintance of the distant Other, and perhaps learn that he or she is not as distant as often assumed.

The Other is a figure that recurs in what follows, and the question of difference is the red thread that runs through the book. Several Others are in play. There is the Other that a given scholarly paradigm can become in the accounts of competing ones. There is the Other news channel (a role played in some accounts by Fox News or Russia Today). There is, crucially, the distant Other—the villain, victim or stranger that populates countless news reports—and the matter of who is cast in the role, and how he or she is depicted.

The key concept of difference is multi-faceted. One focus in this book is the difference between channels that all speak to a global audience in English, but which are based in different parts of the planet and in different cultural settings. Another is how different parts of the world are represented in the output of those channels, to the extent that they are at all. A third and crucial difference concerns how journalists working for these channels deal with diversity. In an age characterized by unprecedented flows of people across state borders—with more adrift from their origins than at any time since the Second World War—the trials of cultural integration in democracies of the once (and still comparatively) affluent 'North', and challenges consequently posed to journalists to represent human diversity without falling back on stereotypes, are daunting, to say the least. How they are met in the day-to-day work of reporting the news to audiences that are everywhere, and yet nowhere in particular, is a matter of considerable concern.

This book is part of the Global Crises and the Media series because the difficulties involved in reporting difference are symptomatic of the larger crisis facing globalized societies. That crisis is reflected in the rise, growth and electoral success of anti-immigration parties and the resurgence of fascism and neo-Nazism in Europe and elsewhere. Instead of extending and deepening cooperation across national borders to meet the challenges that transgress them, confidence in political projects like the European Union (EU) has waned, and voices calling for withdrawal from it and for the repatriation of problem-solving have become increasingly influential. The crisis is one of representation, which matters to shared understandings of common, imperiled futures.

The context of inquiry

The World News Prism, a leading textbook on global news (its 8th edition was published in 2011) tells its readers that a new global society 'of sorts' is emerging 'rapidly and inexorably', but that many nations, especially in the Middle East and Africa, do not feel part of it. What the authors call 'institutions of transnational communication' (but also, variously, 'international' and 'global' media) are helping make this happen. The reporting of the war against the Taliban and the Iraq conflict, they write, serve as reminders 'of how much we have become a global society'. *Time* and *Newsweek*, it is noted, have international editions; businessmen in many nations read the *Financial Times* and *The Economist*, 'and CNN and BBC World are viewed in almost every country'. Africa is presumably an exception, given that it is 'beset by economic stagnation, drought and famine, political unrest and corruption, and brutal civil wars', with many African countries now 'failed nations' (Hachten & Scotton 2007: xviii–xx).

It is a typical account, that positions Anglo-Saxon perspectives, output, audiences, and scholarship at the self-evident centre of analysis. Global media studies are often not so global. In scholarship as in 'reality' there are global divides (Pieterse 2009).

Cottle & Rai (2008c) are among those who have noted that the field of study is structured by competing paradigms and theoretical perspectives. They are right, although 'fractured' is perhaps a better word than 'structured', and 'empirical' could be added to 'theoretical'. McMillin (2007) distinguishes between four general research approaches. A substantial literature provides largely descriptive historical accounts of international communication; critical political economists 'document the phenomenal power and reach of global media empires'; textual analyses examine the volume and content of media flows; and reception studies using surveys and ethnographic analyses seek to assess the implications of those flows for viewers, listeners and readers (McMillin 2007: 9). This work is seen as being largely biased towards Western theories and media structures, which are inappropriate to an era of globalization, and concerned with the media industry—understood to be capitalist and based in the West—rather than the lived experiences of the people throughout the world who make and consume the news, and the stories they have to tell.

As with globalization itself, some view technological, economic and institutional developments in terms of continuity rather than change—as the latest chapter in a story begun in the age of imperialism, at the end of the 19th century (Robertson 2015). Others look out of the ivory tower and see something radically new. The 'transformation of the media', according to Stevenson (1999), is one of the most important social changes facing advanced societies, and has profound implications for 'our shared world', because media flows put us in touch with the lives of people we have never met. Another central debate identified by scholars in the field has to do with what Dencik (2013) designates 'the changing nature of political space and scale in the contemporary system'. In the global space, the nature of representation necessarily changes. This is an evolution that scholars belonging to the 'global turn' in studies of political community, citizenship and communication have sought to grasp.

More prosaically, journalism research has, over the past five decades, looked for and presented a variety of explanations of why news reports convey the versions of the world that they do. A mystical force referred to by mediatization theorists as 'media logic' haunts many accounts, while journalists themselves have described the often unwritten rules of the newsroom more bluntly. In the early days of the satellite revolution, AP correspondent Rosenblum lamented that

> Each person who reports foreign news is part of a process which is riddled with failings, beset by obstacles and tailored largely to wheedle attention from a public assumed to be apathetic and only mildly literate. This system is geared as much to amuse and divert as it is to inform (Rosenblum 1993: 2).

A senior BBC journalist was quoted in one study as saying that programme editors—even in public service broadcasting—are driven by audience interest, and that audiences are not interested in the developing world (Philo 2004: 4). A journalist who has covered the world for Swedish television gives the 'dramaturgy of the media, whereby a news story is almost always a negative event, a problem or a crisis' as the reason why Western media have entirely missed the fact that many countries on the African continent have quietly undergone a dynamic development since the mid-1990s (Bjerström 2013: 12).

As is well known, Galtung and Ruge found, in the 1960s, that journalists' decisions as to which foreign events to report were determined by factors such as the geographical and cultural proximity of the country in focus to the reporting country, and its elite status or otherwise (Galtung & Ruge 1965). Subsequent studies have built on this notion of proximity (see for example Kariel & Rosenvall (1983) and Kim & Barnett (1996)) and documented a variety of proximity-related determinants. Economic determinants are one sort. A study by Rosengren (1974) that showed a positive correlation between the volume of trade and the volume of reporting on trade countries in German, Dutch and British newspapers, continues to be cited in this context. Another determinant is the presence of international (i.e. Western) news agencies (Wu 2007). Other studies have found that certain traits make it more or less likely that a given country will feature in the news reports of another. Determinants of foreign news coverage identified in the literature include geographical or population size (Wu op. cit.), government policy, national interest and foreign policy orientation of the reporting country (Riegert 1998; Kim et al. 2007; Cohen 2013) and its colonial ties (d'Haenens & Verelst 2002) or, conversely, the standing of the country that is the focus of reports (Mowlana 1997; Chang et al. 2000) and its cultural or political significance (Lee 2005; Shoemaker 1996). Freeman (2010: 273) notes that research on the determinants of foreign news has tended to focus on reporting of individual countries, rather than world regions. The contributors to an anthology edited by Cohen (2013) identified superpower status, neighbourhood, and incidence of violent conflict as determining features. Importantly, the study found that while the incidence of wars and disaster increased the likelihood of a given country being included in television news reports, it made audiences less likely to watch.

Despite the empirical substance of many of these studies, Willnat & Martin (2012: 504) are justified in saying that research on foreign news reporting and, not least, the people who do it, has tended to be 'overly descriptive, usually atheoretical, or produced results that lacked contributions to theory-building'. Scholars joining the conversation from another direction have contributed more to the theoretical discussion. It has been noted that governments' public relations efforts can influence news accounts of world politics (Lee 2007), but this is not just a matter of 'nation-branding': Roselle, Miskimmon, & O'Loughlin (2014) argue that 'strategic narratives' are an increasingly important tool in a 'chaotic world' run by leaders who are 'ill-prepared for its complexities'. Narratives 'explain the world and set constraints on the imaginable and actionable and shape perceived interests'; they can be 'a power resource setting out what characterizes any state in the world, or how the world works'. Such narratives work on three inextricably linked levels. On the level of the international system are narratives which describe how the world is structured, how it works, and who makes it work. On the national level, stories are told about the values of the state in international relations, while narratives on the issue level 'set governmental actions in a context' (Roselle et al. 2014: 76). Cottle and Rai (2008a) have also written of the importance of narrative structures, which they conceive of as 'communicative frames'. In distinction to techniques used by political actors such as governments and states, communicative frames are 'firmly anchored in the world of television newswork and production'. What Cottle and Rai have in mind are overarching ways of seeing and telling that prevail in a given newsroom culture, rather than the structure of a particular news item (which is a more common use of the word 'frame'). In this broader sense, the communicative frame resembles the 'newsroom narrative' or 'myth' seen at work in other newsroom studies (Robertson 2010: 50–57). By drawing attention to this phenomenon, Cottle and Rai raise larger questions about the 'communicative architecture' of television journalism, and how it structures the 'wider play of power, culture and contention' (2008a: 94). An intriguing question is whether the global newsroom has a communicative architecture that is distinctive from the national settings on which the account of Cottle and Rai is based (India and South Africa), and if so, whether that distinctive global culture makes a difference to accounts of the world.

Entering the global newsroom

'Global news' is a key concept in the study reported here: it forms, after all, part of the title of the book. But what exactly is it? Wasserman (2011: 102) has argued that a good deal of scholarly reorientation and theorization is needed to make sense of the phenomenon represented by a word (global) that is often used without sufficient thought in news contexts. As mentioned above, this book's structuring principle is the notion of worlds, in plural, to distance the account from the abstract phenomenon customarily treated as something relatively homogenous, or as something vague, described by Clausen (2003), for example, as reports of global topics, crafted for audiences anywhere, that lack distinctive traits. Nor is it helpful to say that global news is something produced by 'the global journalist', if that actor is the one described in a recent worthy tome (Weaver & Willnat 2012). That comparative study concerns journalists in 33 different countries throughout the world, reporting to 33 national audiences—people with quite different remits from journalists reporting for global audiences. Nor is global news assumed here to be synonymous with 'international', 'transnational' or 'foreign' news—terms which are often used interchangeably within the same text (Malek & Kavoori 1999; Berger 2009). Gunaratne (2007) distinguishes between them, however. Observing that the term 'international communication fails to capture what scholars in the field actually study', he defines transnational communication as non-governmental exchanges that transcend national boundaries, and global communication as interactions involving all nations (Gunaratne 2007: 268. See also Wessler et al. 2008 for an explication of the different dimensions of transnationalism).

Some, like Hafez, have questioned whether such a thing as global journalism does, or indeed can, exist.

> We cannot yet talk of global journalism as a form of successful, plural and diversified communication. There are, at best, various zones of transnationality, a western, an American, a European, Muslim, Arab or whatever sphere, with different narratives, frames, master-frames of the same story (Hafez 2011: 486–7).

This is a moot point (finding even common European frames can be a challenge). The observation is apparently not based on empirical engagement with such narratives, and is not particularly helpful when it comes to thinking about what global journalism does in fact entail. Scholars who conceive of global news not in terms of selecting, but of telling, have more to offer here, by paying attention to whether stories about a particular issue are framed as having a foreign or global dimension (Berger 2009). Clausen (2003) argues that the only thing universal about news is that it is domesticated everywhere: global news is different, or particular, in every country. Dencik found that global news had a pronounced British accent in the BBC World newsroom. Her fieldwork showed that

> dependence on political rhetoric from dominant political powers is deeply rooted in the domestic journalistic culture of BBC news workers that, in producing simultaneously across BBC news outlets, is translated onto a global canvas. That is to say, 'globality' comes to be representative of a specific understanding of legitimacy and credibility that is embodied within a specific cultural context of news production [...] When asked about the difference in covering a story for a domestic outlet versus a global outlet, the vast majority of those interviewed did not consider there to be a major difference between the two and said that any changes to news reports are merely cosmetic, such as adding 'British' in front of a reference to the Prime Minister (Dencik 2013: 10).

Being anchored in a specific domestic setting need not hinder journalism from being global. Berglez (2008, 2013) argues that its defining feature is neither the site of the newsroom nor its targetting of a non-national audience, but a particular mindset. Global journalism happens when reporters and editors show how issues are 'embedded in global processes, that is, when cognitively and discursively conjuring up a globalizing society' (2013: 2). Berglez finds global journalism in Swedish newsrooms, and while this is the only place he looks for it, he maintains that global journalism is not what is practiced in global newsrooms. Rather, it is

> a global discursive news movement which develops from "below", i.e., not in the editorial milieus of Al Jazeera and BBC World but in hundreds of thousands of local and national news media (Berglez 2013: 21, 125).

Berglez is both right and wrong. He is right in saying that global journalism is about outlooks and the ambition—coupled with the ability—to explain to local, national, or other audiences that a given issue can only be understood in the context of globalization, i.e. as part of the intermingling of economies, people and problems. But to suggest that global journalism can only develop from below, and to dismiss the work done in newsrooms targetting global audiences by journalists at home everywhere and nowhere, is to miss an important point—or several, as this book will attempt to show.

Berglez is not the only one to think of news reporting in terms of discursive power, just as he is far from alone in thinking that some journalistic endeavours can foster a sense of the world as a singular, shared space, stimulating awareness not only that viewers have connections with people elsewhere, but also making it possible 'to imagine the world as a whole' (Halsall 2006: 8; Cottle 2009).

A variety of authors have devoted some thought into this sort of power. Some wear what Hannerz (2004) would call a worried face, because of concerns that people's imaginations are being shaped by corporate interests. Some, like Pieterse, wear a frustrated expression. From their post at the ivory tower window, they observe the 'rise of the Rest', but can also see that it is underestimated and under-represented in 'mainstream media', which frame that rise as a threat or ignore it 'because it doesn't fit national narratives in the West' (Pieterse 2009: 222; 231). Some have a more optimistic visage (Cheah 2013; Meskimmon 2012; Morley & Robins 1995; Orgad 2012; Shaw 2012; Shohat & Stam 1994; Siapera 2010; Stevenson 1999, 2003; Tomlinson 1999, 2011; Urry 2002). Scholars gazing out of a window overlooking fertile cosmopolitan fields keep returning to Silverstone (2007), who used the notion of 'mediapolis' to think about how the media structure relations between self and other in global spaces. Silverstone argued that the world's media form a site of increasing importance to the construction of a moral order that grows alongside global interdependence. Technologies and discourses 'define a space that is increasingly mutually referential and reinforcive, and increasingly integrated into the fabric of everyday life', he maintained (Silverstone 2007: 6). This matters to the prospects for getting along in an interdependent world, because when media actors and outlets provide frameworks for the appearance of the

Other, they define the moral space in which the Other appears to us, and invite 'an equivalent moral response from us, the audience, as a potential or actual citizen' (2007: 7).

On television

This book is not about global media: it is about global television. The turbulent times documented by the newsrooms in focus here have been punctuated by events often been referred to as 'Twitter' and 'Facebook revolutions', and considerable attention has been paid to the part played by social media in mobilizations sparked by the global economic crisis (Bennett & Segerberg 2012; Bimber 2012; Robertson 2015: 84–98). In 2013, an entire special issue of *Journalism Studies* was devoted to cosmopolitanism and the new news media, and to how social media have allowed 'ordinary voice' to intervene and engender a 'new authenticity' that catalyses cosmopolitanism (Chouliaraki & Blaagaard 2013). Social media are thus on the frontlines of both research and global politics. Why then study television?

The point of departure for this study is that television continues to be relevant, and that there is a need to study it systematically and imaginatively. In the rush to make sense of the political impact of media developments, the impression is often given that established media actors and institutions remain constrained by old practices and hampered by traditional role conceptions and technological forms. But social media are not by default those that matter most either in contemporary mediations of crisis or in wider understandings of politics. As one of the news executives interviewed later in this book pointed out, internet penetration is low in regions his global organization is very interested in reaching,[1] and television viewing has actually increased in places where people have ready access to social media, such as most European countries (Eurodata 2014). The global channels whose worlds are explored in these pages have survived and in some cases flourished in the period that has seen social media burgeon and come to dominate the literature on political communication. The channel that plays a leading role in what follows—Al Jazeera English—began operations after the launching of Twitter, so is 'newer' than 'new' media even if only chronologically. More importantly, television is now all media technologies combined. Forget the box in the living room. The channels studied in this book broadcast their programmes on YouTube, and their news reports are often consumed in the form of written articles posted online. Some television correspondents are on Twitter more often than they are on camera, and the channels they work for make and broadcast films and documentaries, as well as news bulletins. The 'television' of global television news channels is thus all things at once—article, website, blog, Twitter feed, Instagram and what McLuhan called the 'hot' medium of film and radio (when disseminated as podcast) as well as the 'cool' medium that people watch while sitting on the couch, remote control in hand, that was still in its infancy in McLuhan's day. Placing global television at the centre of analysis—understanding it as what Castells (2009) would call a 'switcher' between national and transnational communication nodes, where 'old' and 'new' media converge—affords an excellent opportunity to study larger issues of representation in changing political and media ecologies.

The imagery and narrative techniques deployed in television journalism are mechanisms which have the potential to bring the world closer to viewers on other continents, and make them comfortable with the diversity that characterizes a world of transborder flows. But the same techniques can do precisely the opposite, and strengthen the instinct to keep the world at arm's length through Othering practices. This brings us to the book's central puzzle. Stereotyping and 'othering' mechanisms are generally thought to be detrimental to democracy, while respect for, and representation of, diversity can be thought to promote it. How do journalists working in global newsrooms conceive of their roles, especially when it comes to reporting 'difference' and 'differently'? What does content tell us about getting the balance 'right'? And in seeking answers to such questions, what can be learned about the crisis of representation referred to at the outset?

Coming up next

Reviewing the literature on international communication more than two decades ago, Stevenson (1992) noted that it contained, on the one hand, polemics with little evidence and, on the other, works that documented interesting features of the field without seeking to explain them. He and others (such as Chang, 1998) identified a need for more interconnections between theoretical and empirical enquiry. It is an enduring need.

There are others. Udupa (2012: 880) has astutely noted that the limitations of media theories 'rooted in the experiences of western democracies' have been thrown into sharp relief by the recent expansion of news media in the globalizing economies of post-colonial societies. Much work is needed, sighs Wasserman (2011: 1010),

> to reorient scholarly production in the field of journalism studies towards a truly global outlook which will take the differentiated practices, institutions and structural conditions of the global South seriously in its theorisation around journalism in the era of media globalisation.

Udupa and Wasserman are among the critics who have rightly observed blind-spots in the media globalization paradigm, according to Waisbord (2013b), who sees it as 'a Rorschach blot of scholarly debates about contemporary trends and dynamics', often taking the form of assertions and hopes, rather than a clear set of questions and theories backed up by empirical evidence.

This book offers empirical answers to several questions of relevance to the debate. What do the people working in global newsrooms tell their audiences about the world, and how do they understand the work that this involves? How appropriate is it to make generalizations about 'global news' and global newsrooms, and what can be learned from comparing them? Finally, how does the view from the ivory tower compare with the view from the newsroom?

The work of four news organizations is explored in an attempt to find answers to these and related questions: two established 'mainstream' broadcasters, based in the Western, and more specifically, Anglo-Saxon world (BBC World and CNN International) and two challengers sometimes referred to as 'counter-hegemonic' media (Al Jazeera English and Russia Today). They are interesting for more than the fact that they reach hundreds of millions of viewers. At a time when most media organizations are slashing their budgets for international reporting, these organizations represent a spectrum of financing solutions and relations to political power. What they all have in common is the espousal by journalists working for them of the purportedly universal values of professionalism and objectivity, and the fact that they all speak to their global audience in English. The focus on English-language broadcasts provides a unique opportunity to gain analytical purchase on a global communicative space that is often invoked, but rarely subjected to empirical analysis—systematic or otherwise.

One of the world's oldest global broadcasters, BBC World (BBCW) is under the remit of the state-funded World Service, although dependent on commercial revenues. While viewer statistics for global operators are not unproblematic, it is safe to say that BBCW is not only one of the world's oldest globals: reaching 388 million households (with fulltime distribution to 249 million) in 2014, it is also one of the most watched.[2] CNN, however, was long emblematic of the global newsroom, and the 'CNN Effect' was for a decade or so the generic term used to refer to media influence on foreign policy. In 2014, CNN International (CNNI) boasted that its services were available 'to more than two billion people in more than 200 countries and territories'.[3] Whereas BBC World News is hosted (from London) by a reasonably large number of different newsreaders, *International Desk* is usually hosted (from Washington) by star anchor Hala Gorani (in the periods studied here and as the book goes to press). Both BBCW and CNNI conform to the liberal or Anglo-American model of media and politics, which entails a professional ethos centred on the principle of objectivity (Hallin and Mancini 2004: 227). They are also the channels that come to mind when reference is made to 'mainstream media' in a global context—and indeed to global media, full stop.

Al Jazeera English (AJE, to be introduced more fully in Chapter 2) falls in between BBCW and CNNI when it comes to viewer statistics. By 2014, eight years after it went on air, AJE was broadcasting to more than 220 million households in over 100 countries, and was one of the most watched news channels on YouTube even before the pro-democracy mobilization of 2011.[4] The name Al Jazeera was associated, until recently, with an Arabic news service popular in the Middle East and diaspora, that became an influential but controversial news source during the Bush administration's war on terror. The research reported here concerns the channel that broadcasts news in English across the globe, around the clock. It operates from the same base in Doha, and is financed the same way (by the ruling al Thani family of Qatar), but differs from the Arabic channel in a number of significant ways. In spite of this, it has yet to attract the same amount of scholarly attention (Seib 2012; Figenschou 2010: 87). Russia Today (RT) started operations shortly before AJE. Funded by the Russian Federal Agency on Press and Mass Communications, it is by most accounts significantly better off than the majority of other Russian media. Like AJE, it carries no advertisements, and many of its reporters and newsreaders are native English speakers, trained in the UK and other parts of the English-speaking world. Again, viewer statistics are difficult to verify, but RT claims to broadcast to 644 million people in more than 100 countries, to have some two million viewers in the UK, where it is available through Freeview (digital terrestrial television); to be the second-most-watched foreign news channel after BBCW in the US, where it reaches 85 million viewers via cable or satellite; and the most-watched news channel on YouTube.[5] RT and AJE both claim to be different from their competitors, and they are. But they differ from each other too, as will be seen.

Surprise is occasionally expressed at the decision to design a study around news organizations payrolled by the Kremlin or the ruling dynasty of an authoritarian state. Wasserman provides a rebuttal, however: whatever the lack of democratic accountability in these institutional contexts, the Western (or Northern) model of media financing is not the only one, and other versions must be taken into consideration, and their output compared, if the preconditions for global journalism are to be appreciated. Further support for this research strategy is provided by Roselle et al. (2014), who point out that the new communication ecology has opened space for 'significant contestation' over different versions of world events, giving rise to the strategic question of whether 'old media stalwarts' like BBCW and CNNI will be able to retain their historical status, reach and influence in the face of new television channels, as well as 'new media'. This book takes a comparative look at the competition, and in so doing contributes empirical substance to the discussions taking place in the ivory tower about newsmaking in the global village.

· 2 ·

COLLIDING WORLDS

'As media are increasingly monopolized, the number of voices interested in bringing their viewers a little something called truth
has decreased. As a result, instead of representing journalism, the media have become loud mouthpieces for corporations.'[6]

The title of this chapter takes its name from a cult science fiction film of 1939, which reflected contemporary concerns about what happens when technology brings alien peoples into direct contact. While such encounters (of a more terrestrial nature) comprise the overarching concern of this book, this chapter looks at other things that collide. One sort of collision considered here is that between corporate interests and the information rights and needs of news audiences throughout the world. Another is the jarring between different funding forms (private, public or state) and between the different political systems in which the newsrooms in this book are based, and in some cases, their backers' soft power agendas. The chapter begins with an overview of critical theoretical perspectives on media globalization, expanding on the discussion sketched briefly in Chapter 1. A closer look is then taken at two channels often said to be challenging the 'hegemony' of global news outlets based in the West: Al Jazeera English (AJE) and Russia Today (RT). The discussion is based on an analysis of narrative themes that emerge from interviews with news executives and journalists conducted in Moscow and Washington in 2011, in Doha and Stockholm in 2012, and in London in 2013.

Critical theoretical perspectives

Gramsci used the word hegemony to conceptualize how the strong dominate not just by physical force, legal coercion or economic advantage, but also through ideology, by shaping how people understand the world, how it works, what the natural order of things is, and where they belong in it. The idea is that, embedded as they are in ideological contexts, those without power play an active role in their own subjugation. Hegemony theory has been used not just to explain how disadvantaged classes consent to their continued subordination by unrepresentative individuals and classes, but also how developing and disadvantaged countries on what Wallerstein (1976, 1990) calls the 'periphery' of the world system submit to exploitation by states of the centre or 'core', which control information as they do other flows. Critical political economists looking out of the ivory tower see the US looming large in the centre of the field of vision, surrounded by the old member states of the European Union and other G8 countries. Large parts of Asia, Latin America and most of Africa—countries referred to as the 'least developed nations', 'developing countries' and the 'Third World', are on the periphery, like the receding landscape in Bruegel's painting.

It is a vintage paradigm, but students in university classrooms the world over continue to be taught that world system theory 'provides the concepts, ideas, and language for structuring international communication' (McPhail 2014: 18). News coverage is analysed from this perspective in terms of the 'ripple effect' expanding outwards from the centre of the world system (Kim & Barnett 1996; Chang 1998), and scholars regularly produce studies said to show that the accounts of the world provided in news reports are 'hegemonic' (Leung 2009: 252). Political scientists, sociologists and media scholars have noted the structural and communicative disparities between countries configured, historically, by colonialism, and subsequently, by the profit-seeking activities of global capitalism (Gerbner & Marvanyi 1977; Wilhoit & Weaver 1983). News about the developing world in particular is 'distorted' because

> the Western press largely reflects the interests of the global business class, especially the financial press, and exhibits a tendency to report only what its readers, the business class, want to see (Rowden 1998-99).

Wallerstein dislikes the concept of globalization, which he has famously called 'meaningless as an analytic concept', but his argument that culture and meaning are shaped by the economic interests of the powerful is central to the academic discourse of cultural globalization. An array of scholars have drawn attention to the emergence, apace with globalization, of giant media companies with a global presence—companies like Disney, General Electric, News Corporation and Time Warner (Hopper 2007:61; Martell 2010:80). These are seen as replicating the same kinds of cultural products on every continent, with cultural homogenization or 'McDonaldization' the result (Martell 2010: 90). Scholars like Bourdieu (1993, 1999), Boyd-Barrett & Rantanen (1998), Herman & McChesney (2000) and McPhail (2014), and policymakers in UNESCO and the EU (Reding 2009; Robertson 2014) have warned that market-driven media globalization is a threat to national autonomy and cultural diversity: as the saying goes, 'rich media' produce 'poor democracy' (Cottle & Rai 2008c; Holly 2008; Kaitatzi-Whitlock 2011). Instead of being addressed as communities of citizens, people are seen as having been transformed by media globalization into global audiences of consumers, organized into niche segments to suit advertisers (Robertson 2015). The venerable concepts of 'cultural imperialism' and 'Americanization' are still used in some accounts to denote this activity, reflecting the tenacious view that US corporate interests are the driving force behind media globalization.

McChesney (2013) uses the word 'oligopoly' to describe the situation that prevails when a few media companies dominate each media sector. These oligarchs exert such control over their market corners that the idea of consumer sovereignty becomes a nonsense: media owners may give people what they want, but only within a fixed range of choice (McChesney 2013: 73–5). The dominant players treat media systems in different countries and continents 'as a single global market with local subdivisions' (Herman & McChesney 2000: 216). McPhail (2014) provides a similar analysis, although his key concept is colonialism rather than oligopoly. His 'Electronic Colonialism Theory' stipulates that global media 'influence how people look, think and act', and that global communication giants spawn 'a shared media culture influencing perceptions and values' (2014: 24).

> The media become a veil of collective news images, which we absorb into our minds and eventually, even if subtly, begin to act out, dress, or speak differently as we consume input from mass media rather than from family, community or former friends. The socialization process is hijacked by the media empires rather than the colonial empires of days gone by (2014: 23).

Media conglomerates, in this view, 'control, reproduce and spread' the global flow of images that work on the minds of the audience 'without regard to geography'. While these media giants may describe themselves as global, critical political economists insist that they are in fact American, and have simply moved beyond borders because the US market is saturated (Van Ginneken 1998). These 'foot soldiers of colonialism' are not merely corporate but indeed imperialist, it is argued:

> Just as the British ruled the world by controlling the seas, so now the United States and a few other core nations rule the airwaves, television and movie screens, mobile media, and the emerging digital universe. The minds of many, without regard to time or space, are clearly influenced by the flow and content of a vast range of core-nation media products (2014: 361).

Thussu is another critical scholar who has expressed concern that the news flowing across national borders is becoming homogenized, in an account of what he calls the globalization of 'infotainment'. In a book that has been reprinted multiple times, Thussu (2009a) writes that this scourge 'can be seen as part of a wider process of corporate colonization', which makes it 'essential to understand the political, economic, military and cultural vectors of neoliberal imperialism' (Thussu 2009a: 134). He describes the tendency of global news broadcasters to resort to entertainment formats and to fill the gaping 24/7 news hole with 'talking heads', and maintains that complex situations are trivialized and sensationalized because of television's need for 'arresting and action-packed visuals and dramatic pictures' (2009a: 113). What he refers to as the 'dominant television news discourse' opts for diversion and 'high-tech infotainment spectacles' rather than deeper analysis of geo-political issues (Thussu 2009a: 132). Granted, on the last few pages of *News as Entertainment*, Thussu observes that media ownership has diversified with the launch of Al Jazeera English, Russia Today, CCTV in China, Telesur in Latin America, France24 and transnational ventures involving Indian television news companies (Thussu 2009a: 176–7). The book nevertheless ends with a sigh.

> Water shortage and sanitation do not make marketable infotainment; pets do, they are cuddly and evoke touchy-feely reactions, and most important, look pretty on television. Global infotainment, a mask for neo-liberal imperialism led by the United States, is transforming television news around the world (Thussu 2009a: 178–9).

Whether or not journalists working for global news organizations agree that their broadcasts are no place for water shortage and sanitation issues is not something generally investigated by critical political economists. Analyses of global media are instead based on ownership statistics and evidence invoked often seems to be the outcome of personal viewing experiences rather than systematic empirical analysis. What do things look like from the perspective of the newsroom, at the metaphorical base of Bruegel's tower, rather than its lofty summit?

'Big business equals bad journalism as corporations control info flow'

The view of the driving forces behind the world's major media companies expressed in the reports of one of the four newsrooms in this study bears a striking resemblance to the account of media power provided by McChesney and echoed by others surveyed above. The quote at the beginning of this chapter is from a typical Russia Today news item. The report, entitled 'Media Monopoly', broadcast on 29 January 2011, is reproduced in some detail below to enable a comparison of the discourse of RT and that of scholarship on critical political economy.

The report begins with the newsreader telling viewers that trust in the media is on the wane in the US, and that 'many' are sceptical about the likelihood that the large corporations that own the networks providing people with unbiased output. 'He who pays the paper gets to call the tune', says the first of four experts enlisted to further the narrative. Clips from interviews with these critics, all edited into brief soundbytes that fit securely into the reporter's storyline, problematise the media monopoly in focus in the news item.[7] The RT reporter in New York explains that the people paying the piper are corporations, and the tune they call is what Americans see, hear and read. 'It's a money-maker', the second expert cuts in, adding that contrary to popular belief, 'the media is the industry of the 21st century'. The reporter goes on to explain that half a century ago, there were as many as 50 corporations running the major networks and newspapers, but that a monopoly situation now prevails. Such concentration is dangerous, because 'it robs democracy of diversity', says a third expert. The reporter adds that 'analysts' (who are not named) say it is 'the golden age of media bias'. News Corporation's Rupert Murdoch is named as the man at the top of the list of owners with conflicts of interest, and one of the experts talks about the partisan bias of Fox News, before the report moves on to name the companies whose spectres haunt the scholarly accounts summarized at the beginning of the chapter.

> General Electric, one of the largest military contractors for the US government, plus Comcast, one of America's largest cable providers, are joined by the hip, running the NBC network [...] CNN and Time Magazine belong to Time Warner. Joining the media giants are CBS Corporation towering over CBS News. And Viacom, a global entertainment company running, among others, Comedy Central. [...] The purpose of existence for corporations is profit, meaning investors' interests are placed ahead of anything else that would matter in journalism. (RT, report entitled 'Media Monopoly', 29 January 2011 newscast)

Like Thussu, one of the experts in the Russia Today report notes it is in effect military contractor General Electric that 'brings us our news about war'. Outspoken radio host Alex Jones explains that 'the old dinosaur media' are now owned by five or six 'mega-conglomerates', who have received secret payments of taxpayer money directly from the the Bush administration to promote federal initiatives. The RT reporter concludes that,

> as the media are increasingly monopolized, the number of voices interested in bringing their viewers a little something called the truth has decreased. As a result, instead of representing journalism, the media have become loud mouthpieces for corporations.

Implicit in the RT critique, and characteristic of its reporting in general, is the implication that this would only happen in the West, and that an alternative voice is needed to counter that Western hegemony.

Contra-flows and counter-hegemonic media

The reason that the bleak account given in *News as Entertainment* (Thussu 2009a) can end with a few words of hope is in focus in an anthology with the same editor, *Media on the Move* (Thussu 2007). Its key concept is 'contra-flow'. The volume opens with a reiteration of concerns about cultural homogenization, but also acknowledgement of a trend towards regionalization, localization and heterogeneity in the global market, and an 'emerging multivocal, global mediasphere'. The possibility is discerned of media power ceasing to be concentrated in the centre, and distributed instead 'among many mini-centres or satraps located in regional hubs'. A new map of global communication is being drawn, in this account. Contributors to the anthology seek to redress an imbalance in scholarship on media globalization which has, they feel, been exclusively concerned with the impact of the Western-global on the non-Western-national (on this topic see also Thussu 2013 and Kupe 2013). The authors express the ambition of exploring the transnational sharing of information and images by 'invisible cosmopolitans' (Georgiou & Silverstone 2007) and of finding out how effective the new contra-flows might be, given that 'their output is relatively small and their global impact largely restricted to the diasporic communities or geo-linguistic constituencies' (Thussu 2007: 4; 11–31).

That there was a need to right information imbalances had been clear for decades by the time the *Media on the Move* anthology appeared in 2007. In the 1970s, there were calls for a 'New World Information and Communication Order', based on the conviction that the hegemony of the rich North and West could be countered by state-backed Third World news agencies (Cottle & Rai 2008c; Berger 2009: 355). Deregulation and the ascent of neo-liberalist market solutions in the 1980s put paid to such plans, insofar as they had existed beyond the recommendations of the MacBride Report (UNESCO 1980). It was not until the new millennium, and more specifically around 2006, that a 'boom' in global news channels became discernible—channels that media analysts like Painter defined as counter-hegemonic because they were established 'with the explicit intention of challenging the "BBC/CNN approach" to world events'—an approach that was not thought to be as neutral, balanced and impartial as it set out to be (Painter 2008: 1). Painter provided a solid, if early, case study of what he identified as two leading counter-hegemonics: AJE and Telesur. The Arabic-language component of the Al Jazeera network has attracted a considerable amount of scholarly attention since its inception (see for example Azran 2004; el-Nawawy & Iskander 2003; el-Nawawy & Powers 2010; Miladi 2006; Wessler & Adolphsen 2008; Wojcieszak 2007; Zednik 2002). Its English sister has, more recently, been the focus of a few studies (see eg. Seib 2012), but the literature is dominated by descriptive and sometimes anecdotal accounts and/or case studies of conflict reporting. The exception is work done by Figenschou (2010, 2011, 2012, 2013) whose interview expeditions to Doha at the beginning of the AJE timeline yielded rich insights. By comparison, scholars have shown little interest in Russia Today, although more attention has been paid to it in the wake of its high and distinct profile in coverage of the Syrian conflict and, from 2014, the Ukrainian crisis. Apart from that, it has inspired a number of critiques by non-academics (see for example Bloomfield 2014; Dzyadko 2014; Freemantle 2011; Heyman 2008; Kiselev 2014; von Twickel 2010).

Al Jazeera English went on air two years after the launch of RT, by which time the Arabic network was firmly established and serving as a textbook example of what Sakr (2007: 116) has called 'the empire striking back'. During the Iraq War, the channel had emerged as a key communicative player (el-Ibiary 2011; Seib 2008; Pintak 2009) and the literature began to contain references to an 'Al Jazeera Effect'—a paraphrase of a term frequently used in the early 1990s, when the Gulf War became the first to be broadcast live on satellite television, and CNN became a household word. But while the 'Al Jazeera Effect' referred to the emergence of a new voice for the Arab world and diaspora, and a transformation in the ethos of Arab journalism (Pintak 2009: 297), it was pointed out that more than superficial changes in 'the geography of media flows' were required for such an effect to be considered evidence of contra-flow. That notion, Sakr (2007: 117) argued, has more analytical purchase when related to programming from the South that is appreciated by local audiences, by migrants, and by host communities in the global North.

But what, more precisely, is a counter-hegemonic medium? What is involved in the business of striking back? And what forces sustain such outlets, if not those of the market? Seen from one vantage point, channels like RT and AJE are manifestations of soft power, no different in this respect from broadcasters like CNN International or BBC World. This perspective sees the media ecology as a battlefield populated by empires striking back and forth. Virilio opined, the year the Berlin Wall came down, that media technologies had taken on the status of military targets in their own right, somehow pushing 'the realm of the symbolic into a new prominence in the conduct of war' (Virilio 1989: 85), something that would prove to be increasingly true in the course of the following two decades. Hillary Clinton, then US Secretary of State, put the idea of symbolic conflict more simply when she famously said, early in 2011, that Al Jazeera was winning the information war. (She had in mind the English-language channel that Americans were watching online.) AJE journalists and news executives readily admit their newsroom exists because it is a powerful weapon in the Qatari arsenal. 'It's a soft power issue' for the ruling dynasty, according to the head of the London bureau, Ben Rayner explains that Al Jazeera protects Qatari interests.

> Qatar is a small country sandwiched between Saudi Arabia and Iran. They've looked at the experience of Kuwait up the coast in the early 90s, being invaded by Iraq, militarily it cannot protect itself, if one of these neighbours chose to attack it. But it has enormous wealth, and has sort of carved out a role for itself as a key regional, diplomatic player… Al Jazeera puts Qatar on the map. It is not a mouthpiece for the Al Thani family or Qatari foreign policy, but it is an example of soft power. And they have their tv channels and tv networks in the same way as the BBC had the World

> Service and the Voice of America. You know, the Voice of America is probably more of a propaganda tool, but nobody ever says, oh, BBC World Service is a British propaganda tool… OK, some may, but is it a propaganda tool or is it a way to keep Britain's profile up in the world? Is that propaganda or is that soft power? There's probably a blurring between the edges of the two, isn't there?'[8]

Seib (2008:14) claims that the Al Jazeera network has become 'both a prototype for the new breed of news organizations appearing around the world and a player in global politics'. He cites one of the journalists behind the launching of France24, Ulysse Gosset, who opined that news channels have become 'part of the global battle in the world', playing a role as important as traditional diplomacy or economic prowess (quoted in Seib 2008: 36). Manheim & Albritton (1984) noted the existence, three decades ago, of a phenomenon they named 'international public relations', and others have subsequently observed an increasing professionalism in the work of governments to put a 'positive spin on a nation's image' (Freeman 2010: 272). Rosenblum, a long-serving foreign correspondent, argued years ago that 'America's world is shaped and defined in Washington', where the politically powerful deploy PR specialists to manage what people know, and how they think about what they know, about international politics (Rosenblum 1993: 5).

The conceptual lens of soft power, then, is certainly a suitable one through which to view the decision taken by political power-wielders in capitals such as Moscow and Doha to back global news outlets like RT and AJE. There are others, however. Shafer puts Hamad bin Khalifa Al Thani in the same category as rich patrons in the US private sphere who have stepped in to 'found, fund or seed' non-profit journalism organizations in recent years. As newspapers die and budgets for deploying correspondents throughout the world are slashed, these alternatively funded outlets are those that have the resources to 'walk the investigative beat'. Shafer refers to such funders as 'the new Medicis', who instead of seeking profits 'want primarily to save the world' (Shafer 2013).

It would seem, then, that there is cause to think carefully and comparatively before generalising about 'the global journalist'. It is an empirical question whether this figure is understood as a purveyor of global infotainment, or as a new breed of gatekeeper, manning the sluice to reverse information flows. Is this person a striker in world soft power matches, an instrument of international public relations, or the relatively autonomous beneficiary of neo-Mediciism? One way of seeking an answer to the question is to establish how the newsworkers themselves perceive their role. The rest of this chapter considers how people working for the two outlets sometimes designated as the leading 'counter-hegemonic' outlets describe their goals and their work, in their own words.

The story of Russia Today is quickly told, partly because it is simpler than that of Al Jazeera English, and partly because there is less material available to the researcher. RT's deputy editor-in-chief Alexey Nikolov, and Head of Media and External Communications, Alina Mikhaleva, agreed to be interviewed in August 2011, and to give an official tour of the Moscow studios. Additional interviews with correspondents and visits to the new Washington news centre did not take place, however, despite repeated requests and promises, so the story reproduced below is very much the official network narrative.

The story of Al Jazeera English requires more space and consideration. Its status as a 'counter-hegemonic' channel is more debatable, its news executives and correspondents more willing to talk about their work, and their answers provide richer material to work with if the aim—as in this case—is to explore and better understand difference in the generic global newsroom. When it comes to source criticism, the views expressed by AJE employees are assumed here to be genuinely held, but they were all conducted on AJE premises, and can thus be considered, following previous research, to reflect 'the narrative of the newsroom' (Robertson 2010).

The story of Russia Today

As mentioned earlier, Russia Today, or RT as it is officially marketed, has broadcast news to a global audience from its Moscow newsroom since 2005. An Arabic service was added later and, in December 2009, broadcasts in Spanish. By late 2011 it had a workforce of about 2000 (including 'drivers and legal and bureaux and accounting') of which some twenty were correspondents, according to Nikolov. The average age of reporters, he says, is around 25.

Established with the aim of improving the image of Russia abroad, RT purports to offer a Russian perspective on global events and what Nikolov calls 'the impartial view on Russia'. It is registered as an autonomous non-profit organization, financed by federal funding. Since its inception, the central figure at RT has been Margarita Simonyan, who was recruited as editor-in-chief when only 25, and is said to have strong ties with the Kremlin. Many RT staffers are Russian, but most of its newsreaders are native English-speakers, and several of its journalists come from Western news organizations. High-profile recruits in recent years include Larry King, who had a show on CNN for 15 years, and WikiLeaks founder and celebrity fugitive Julian Assange, host of the eponymous *The Julian Assange Show* (http://assange.rt.com). Assange has been quoted as saying that RT allows guests to say things they 'could not say on a mainstream TV network'.[9] While there is evidence to support this claim, former RT employees have testified to the fact that there are things that cannot be said on RT either. James Freemantle is one such journalist.

> Within a week of arriving, I learned that although we covered many big stories in the region and around the world, when it came to politics, conflict and international relations, Russia Today was little more than a conduit for Kremlin propaganda. If something went to air that seemed likely to offend the sensibilities of Messrs Putin or Mevedev it was immediately pulled and Simonyan would throw a tantrum. Those responsible could be officially reprimanded. Russian journalists would be fined for 'errors'. (Freemantle 2011)

The questions Freemantle asked during live interviews were scripted by Russian journalists, he said, and important stories were never covered, not for lack of resources, 'but because we were told by Simonyan, via Nikolov, that we would not be reporting them'. Vladimir Putin gave a different version of RT autonomy when he visited the newsroom in June 2013.

> When we designed this project back in 2005 we intended introducing another strong player on the international scene, a player that wouldn't just provide an unbiased coverage of the events in Russia but also … try to break the Anglo-Saxon monopoly on the global information streams. And it seems to me that you're succeeding in this job. I'd like to emphasise something of key importance. We never expected this to be a news agency or a channel that would defend the position of the Russian political line. We wanted to bring an absolutely independent news channel to the news arena. Certainly the channel is funded by the government… but I'd like to underline again that we never intended this channel, RT, as any kind of apologetics for the Russian political line, whether domestic or foreign.[10]

Although the idea was 'to bring a Russian voice to the international media chorus', Nikolov claims that its reporting is neutral and objective, and that on many issues 'there is no thing as a Russian side'.

RT is widely acknowledged (for example by the well-renowned Pew Research Institute) to be the most popular news channel on YouTube. Income from advertising is intentionally kept very low, according to Nikolov, distinguishing it from other channels. This is one reason RT has attracted so many viewers, he claims: people get to see 'different stories, different voices, nice girls, no advertising. It's nice to watch, it's fun to watch'. Pure information fails to attract a wide audience, so at RT an attempt is made to find a balance 'between a different take on today's hot story and some nice human story and some idiotic feature, which people will like'.

When pressed on the question of what having a 'different' angle from the 'Anglo-Saxon monopoly' entails in practice, Nikolov declines to elaborate. As for diversity, the Deputy Editor-in-Chief says RT is 'the most international news TV channel in the world', with people of 35 different nationalities. But this was a potential problem, rather than a resource.

> Whenever you have different cultures, mixing and counteracting, you have to hope that in each particular…conflict, there is enough wisdom from two sides and sometimes from the third side and sometimes from the fourth side who interferes so that people eventually…um, bring their cultural differences to a sort of compromise. (Alexey Nikolov, RT Deputy Editor-in-Chief)

As will be seen, this response is in sharp contrast to that given by AJE news executives and journalists. It is one of many points of difference between the channels.

The story of Al Jazeera English

According to its official publications and website, AJE is a 'truly global', news and current affairs channel with a mandate to provide depth and context when reporting about 'the transformative changes taking place across the globe'.[11] It has experienced difficulties with gaining a foothold in the US cable system (Usher 2011), but claims to broadcast to more than 260 million households in over 130 countries, and during the 2011 uprisings in Tunisia and Egypt, it attracted a wide online audience in the US as well as elsewhere, with its web traffic rising 2500%. Like RT, it claims to be the most diverse newsroom in the world, with more than 1000 'highly experienced staff' (not counting the drivers and accountants included in the RT figure) with more than 50 nationalities deployed in the main news centres in Doha and London in and 70 bureaus across the globe.[12] It too has a YouTube channel, launched in 2007, and in 2012 had 443 million video views and over one billion watched minutes on its live stream. Like those of many other broadcasters, its reports can be followed on Facebook, Twitter, podcast, mobile app and SMS alert. The funding for the English channel, which has won numerous international awards for its news coverage and documentaries,[13] comes in the form of state grants. In this respect it bears a greater affinity to the BBC than to RT or CNNI. And like the BBC, AJE is governed by Ofcom (the UK Office of Communications) regulations. Unlike RT, it has an easily accessible code of ethics that is often invoked. Its first article pledges AJE journalists to adhere to the journalistic values of honesty, courage, fairness, balance, independence, credibility and diversity, giving no priority to commercial or political considerations over professional ones. Perhaps the article of most interest here is the sixth, which obliges the channel to

> recognise diversity in human societies with all their races, cultures and beliefs and their values and intrinsic individualities in order to present unbiased and faithful reflection of them.[14]

Interviews (to recapitulate) were conducted with twelve people from various parts of the organization—from executive producer to correspondent—in Doha, London, Washington and Stockholm. Two things are striking about these conversations. One is the individuality of responses: where stock phrases occurred, they tended to be used in quotation marks, marking a certain distance. The other is that these individual views were combined with agreement, expressed by people with quite different cultural backgrounds, regarding the important traits of the news organization they work for. Some of the themes to emerge from the interviews relate to questions explored later on in the book, and will be saved for those discussions. Three themes will be highlighted for the purposes of the present chapter: what it means to do global news; the question of difference (being different from mainstream or 'hegemonic' media, and diversity in the workplace and news reports); and the narrative strategies employed when following the stipulations of Article 6 and in 'reporting the world back to itself', as an AJE advert expressed the organization's ambition in the first week of operations.

The AJE respondents in this study all emphasized that they were working for a global network, with 'a genuinely global audience', different from organizations targetting a domestic audience, or focussing on a specific region. One news executive in Doha found this simplified matters.

> Although we're very geographically wide, I think our rationale is quite simple… it transcends cultures, languages and other things… Exposing injustice is a global theme. It doesn't apply to one particular country or society.[15]

Another found that having a global remit made the work freer. 'I don't have to worry about whether this is going to sell in Dubuque, Iowa', he said. All that matters is whether it is a good story.[16] On the other hand, several respondents found that speaking to the world, rather than interesting the folks in Iowa, made their work more challenging.

> The challenge of reporting to a global audience starts right from the word go. You choose a story and then you think: would this interest a refugee in Yemen? Would it interest the mother of four kids in Vietnam? Is it something that's going to put someone in Europe on the edge of their seat?... You're reporting to no ethnic group or nationality...I think of different people in different places. I think of an immigrant in Norway, I think of a refugee in Yemen, I think of a tycoon in a different part of Europe.[17]

What this means in practice was illustrated by the example of covering the World Economic Forum. Instead of standing in Davos and talking to economic and political elites about, Africa policy, for example, AJE is more likely to deploy correspondents to talk to Africans about the Davos agenda.

'Being global is being local,' said one interviewee, who explained this meant resisting the temptation to over-simplify. 'We make the local international', said another. 'That's what we do. Really well.'[18] There was a considerable degree of unanimity that this ambition is achieved through 'character-driven' narratives that enable viewers to understand how the world looks when seen through someone else's eyes—through Everyman's eyes. The first thing in 'the package' should not be the reporter speaking to camera, as one executive put it. 'We want to hear from the people first, and reporters second'.[19] It was a recurrent theme in the narrative of the AJE newsroom.

> We aim to get to voices other people don't hear. We're in a very good place to hear from people who are directly related to the story, rather than politicians and NGOs, because we are on the ground in all sorts of places and we can get first-hand to the refugee camp or the village... We have a particular emphasis on trying to talk to people, trying to get to people.[20]

> When other networks go to the summit, where there are heads of state, we might ignore it or cover it in a limited way, but go and find stories about some of the issues which are being debated at the summit which are affecting the lives of ordinary people. We move away from 'high helicopter issues' that the state, prime ministers, presidents want to talk about...our fundamental rationale is that we really want to hear from people in the world who have something to say but don't have the channel or means of saying it.[21]

> You feel that you can't get too far in, you can't get your hands dirty enough, that's the feeling. There's much less reliance on announcements from senior figures. We like to hear it from the people who are in the teeth of it, rather than going to the guys in the comfortable offices. We'd rather go to people and ask: what's it like?... Get to people who haven't ever been listened to and let them say something that other people will hear.[22]

> When our reporters go in they speak to the people. To you, a mother; to me, a father; to a school teacher, a boy, a victim of rape, a victim of shrapnel, somebody who lost their feet.[23]

Such reporting strategies are related, in these responses, to the fact that the Al Jazeera English newsroom is ethnically diverse. A newsreader with decades of experience working for other organizations said this meant he found himself thinking differently.[24] Simply being surrounded by people from many cultures engenders respect for others, a sense of tolerance and understanding for 'other people and other thoughts, other beliefs, other opinions' that 'bleeds into the stories', according to one executive.[25] The organization's diversity is its greatest strength, explained another, who told about having walked into countless meetings, thinking he was abreast of affairs, only to be told by a staffer with local knowledge of India (for example) that a small blurb in a regional newspaper was actually a big story. 'They'd just educated an entire room full of editors', he laughed, by explaining to them why that Indian story was global news. He said that such local knowledge was recognized as a resource and that it was 'seized on'. This was another recurrent theme.

> You quite often have people saying—they're from New Zealand or they're from Somalia or they're from Sweden or wherever—and they say, 'hang on, this story we're doing, I thought it was about my country and you're getting it wrong!'.[26]

As one producer pointed out, it is not just a matter of which stories to put in the broadcast. The diversity of the AJE workforce—the fact that correspondents are not 'parachuted in from London or DC'—has 'a significant impact on people's sensibilities, on how they interpret stories, analyse stories, write stories, report them'.[27]

Being different, and dealing with difference, is something that the people working in the AJE newsroom work on every day, said the London-based executive. A considerable amount of time is invested in discussing what stories to cover and how to cover them for a global audience, and how to make AJE's reporting of a papal resignation or national election in a European country relevant to viewers everywhere. What makes Al Jazeera different from other global broadcasters, he said, is telling stories from different places, giving them more time and doing them more in-depth. As this journalist and several of his colleagues acknowledged, it is a strategy that places more demands on the audience: 'we are quite wordy, and our story count is very high, so you have to concentrate compared to other networks', said a Doha-based presenter, adding that there were fewer opportunities 'to be warm or humorous to the other side'.[28]

Worlds apart?

'You can compare BBC to Al Jazeera, you can compare Russia Today to CCTV. But you cannot compare the four to each other', said one AJE executive.[29] Comparative analysis of output confirms this. The newsroom interviews also revealed that AJE news staff view BBCW as their counterpart. Both BBCW and AJE are considered public service in spirit, if not in formal constitution; both are governed by Ofcom; and staff migrate between the two companies. AJE respondents did not express the same affinity for RT—quite the opposite, in fact.

> We have a level of objectivity that you don't get from Russia Today. I shouldn't talk about ourselves in the same breath as them. Because I don't consider them rivals or on the same level… Russia Today is in some ways incredibly slick…sometimes it can be quite fun, certainly counter-hegemonic! But it is a Kremlin mouthpiece.[30]

The deputy editor-in-chief of RT, on the other hand, compares his organization to CNN. But another comparison more readily suggests itself. Given its similar preoccupation with the US audience and politics, the avuncular manner of many of its anchors, the scathing tone adopted in many reports, and a predilection for what Nikolov referred to as 'idiotic' human interest stories, RT is curiously reminiscent of Fox News.

RT and AJE are also noticeably different from each other when it comes to journalistic autonomy. In contrast to the sort of control witnessed by Freemantle, AJE newsworkers say there is considerable debate as to what the organisation is 'about' and what it should be doing, and that this is encouraged.

> We try to encourage a democratic attitude. One of our slogans is the voice of the voiceless, so when we're having meetings, people are supposed to be allowed to speak up […] We try to encourage our reporters to be questioning and difficult and awkward,

> and if they're questioning of authority when they're in the field then they're liable to be that way about the decision-making process.

The journalist contrasted the situation prevailing in the AJE newsroom, where the leading stories are 'up for grabs', with the one he encountered when working for a UK broadcaster. At ITN, he knew before coming into work each day which eight or ten stories were going to be covered, because they were the same ones being covered on the BBC or Sky News.

Dencik's study of the BBC World newsroom provides useful material for comparison here. BBCW's 'global' news agenda is set in London, she found, and its news values are firmly anchored in the British domestic political culture. The 'organizational ethos' of the BBC ensures that its journalists are aware of how news is understood and treated within the organization, without any direct influence being exerted from the top. Dencik (2013:8) quotes a correspondent as saying 'the BBC does speak with one collective voice—a voice that has a UK accent and speaks a distinct language. One of the correspondents interviewed for the present study, who had worked for the BBC before migrating to AJE, corroborated this, and recounted being told privately that

> at the BBC there is a BBC-Palestinian line, that we've all agreed to and we stick to, and there is a BBC-Israeli line that we've all agreed to, that we stick to, and we don't question it, and if you question it too much they will sack you, they don't like the boat being rocked… When you work at the BBC it is the British empire broadcasting still, and the focus…is very British-centric.[31]

Dencik's first-hand account of the BBCW newsroom also establishes that it is characterized by 'practices that are set within a specific cultural context'. Newsgathering and the location of bureaus throughout the world reflect the British colonial legacy and adhere to patterns of 'longterm geopolitical significance'(Dencik 2013:9).

In this, and its special focus on the US market, BBCW is comparable to RT. AJE, on the other hand, has no domestic service to piggyback on. When coupled with a budget that is more generous than that of many other news organizations, this means it can give fuller coverage to stories that are too far down in the bulletin for BBCW or CNN to invest in. The journalists and producers interviewed at AJE also expressed the conviction, in different ways, that AJE goes to greater pains to show audiences the consequences of government foreign policies, as compared to London-based journalists working for

CNN and the BBC. These (according to a Doha-based English newsreader who worked for the BBC for many years, as well as for CNN) are 'fed a line by the UK government' and 'report it as fact without questioning it'. One of AJE's Middle East correspondents expressed criticism of the consequences of such approaches.

> Most Americans have absolutely no idea what the consequences of their government's foreign policy has been, they have absolutely no idea about the reality on the ground of their unquestioned support for Israel, they have no idea of what the impact of the Iraq conflict has been, how it has actually radicalized more Muslims on the brink than it's pulled into the Western way of seeing things. They don't see it because their own news organizations don't take them to where the impact is, and actually say that 'the consequence of this decision was X'. … You know the amnesia of Western media, especially American media, you never get to find out how the story ends, because they want to move on.[32]

The governments whose line is reported unquestioningly by BBCW and CNN, in these narratives, are at any rate democratic ones. What relations to state power are in evidence in Moscow and Doha newsrooms? Two contrasting images can serve as heuristics for thinking about the differences. On 7 May 2014, at the height of tensions between the Ukraine and Russia, RT newsreaders and reporters appeared on camera wearing the St. George ribbon, which was being used by the pro-Russian separatists in the Ukrainian conflict. While the RT website explained that wearing the ribbon was like wearing a red poppy in the UK (to honour those who had sacrificed their lives for the nation), the ribbon had just been banned by the Ukrainian parliament. The same week, an image appeared on the AJE website and in its programming, showing row upon row of its correspondents silenced by a cross of black tape across their mouths. Under the slogan 'journalism is not a crime', the image was a protest against a state crackdown on the reporting of political opposition. The specific target was the government in Egypt, where three Al Jazeera staffers were on trial—and subsequently sentenced to seven and ten years in prison—for 'falsifying news'. Their arrests, trial and prison sentences sparked international condemnation, and were widely seen as reprisals for what the Egyptian government perceived as Al Jazeera support for the Muslim Brotherhood. In contrast to the symbolic action of the RT newsreaders and reporters, the AJE protest was supported by journalists working for rival organizations political leaders in many countries condemned the sentence (Saeed 2014). These images, in different ways, illustrate worlds in collision.

The critical scholarly perspectives with which this chapter opened reflect concerns that global news is an increasingly homogenous product, driven by corporate profit incentives, and fashioned to entertain domestic audiences rather than inform and engage global publics. This chapter has considered the approach taken by two organizations established to challenge the global mainstream or, as is sometimes put, 'Western hegemony' in news coverage. In the RT narrative, providing audience members with an alternative viewpoint and enjoining them to 'question more', as the slogan on its website puts it (http://rt.com), means giving pride of place to voices and views critical of Anglo-Saxon capital. There is, in other words, a striking resemblance between the RT critique of power in general and the media in particular, and that of the critical political economists.

This anti-capitalist critique does not figure at all in interviews with news executives and journalists at AJE, but offering a different view of the world is nevertheless a central theme in their accounts. Being different, according to the AJE newsroom narratives, has to do with seeing the world from viewpoints not usually represented by mainstream news organizations. Diversity comes from listening to 'the people on the ground', on the one hand, and, on a more instrumental level, to ensuring that the workplace is populated by people from different cultures. An unanticipated finding is that with a valorization of cultural diversity comes a more even gender balance. The person who follows AJE closely will be struck by how more often a female face addresses them from a conflict zone or crisis-afflicted region, than in both RT, BBCW and CNNI, and by how often correspondents put a microphone in front of a woman, be she elite decisionmaker or migrant worker. Respondents consistently appeared surprised when asked whether this reflects AJE policy: it seemed not to have occurred to them. Having more women populate the newsworld is, it would seem, something that follows naturally when cultural diversity in the newsroom is considered not a potential source of conflict (as at RT), but as a resource. 'It's a rather nice Darwinian thing, isn't it?' said a woman who spends much of her time reporting from hot spots. 'As long as we don't get killed too fast.'[33]

When AJE was still a channel-in-the-making, its managing director at the time, Nigel Parsons, said that the ethos behind Al Jazeera International (as it was originally called) was to treat every news item as effectively a 'foreign story' (Sakr 2007: 120). The interviews excerpted here reveal something else. What comes across is an approach to covering the world that treats every news item as a local story, rather than foreign news. This is a key strategy in the work of AJE journalists to reverse the flow—one with consequences for the sort of news that is reported, and for the questioning of enduring news stereotypes. As one correspondent put it,

> I come from a continent that has been on the receiving end of the Western media, which has always covered famine, deaths, diseases, floods. That's the only time Africa used to make the news. Today, I cover Africa, and those stories, but apart from that, I also cover the successes of Africa and Africans. I am telling the stories of my continent to the people who are used to media outlets bringing them stories about Africa. In essence, we're taking to the living rooms of Western capitals a story that they are not used to. We are effectively reversing the flow of information.[34]

What is needed, reflected a correspondent who expressed a keen awareness of the visual and emotional power of television,

> is to explain to people who have not yet got it, the universality of human nature and aspiration. The more you work in this field, and the more you travel, you realize, we're all the same, one millimetre under the skin.

The challenge of reporting global news lies between conflict and cosmopolitanism, in this view. The task of the journalist is to share an understanding of why things matter—to speak to someone who may come from 'a poverty-stricken middle-class household in suburban Delhi' and explain why they need to care about Syria, as it was put. That sort of storytelling involves two sorts of explanation. It means helping the viewer understand why and how the ripples of that conflict could wash up on their shore too. And it means explaining 'how like you this person is, and how this person's suffering could have been yours'.[35] These journalists see themselves as having the opportunity to report like this because they have resources that others lack, and because they don't have to worry about the whims of domestic audiences—or those of the companies targetting those audiences with advertising. While BBC World, AJE and RT are all dependent, to a greater or lesser extent, on state funding, it is the first two of these that come across, not as 'the global journalist', but as 'the global public broadcaster'. One of these is rooted in a country with an imperial past, while the other seems to provide 'news from nowhere'. These different moorings, in turn, make a difference. To assume the media are American, as Tunstall (1977) once did (but no longer does), and to base conclusions about global communication flows on that assumption, is to miss important insights, if not the point.

· 3 ·

A WORLD IN CRISIS

Atlas Reports

'Al Jazeera has historically had a higher threshold for gore than BBC has, BBC worries about offending its viewers, and in my view it often sanitized all the impact out of its package, because they don't want to upset people too much.
So you know, there are horrible things happening out there, I want people to understand that, I want them to see it'.[36]

The giant Atlas has carried the world on his shoulders, iconographically, from the days of the ancient Greeks to the present. Ayn Rand borrowed the image for the title of her dystopian classic, *Atlas Shrugged.* The novel is a paean to her philosophy of 'objectivism', the central tenet of which is that people have a moral responsibility to put their own self-interests first, and that laissez-faire capitalism is consequently the only acceptable social system. The setting of the 1957 narrative—which continues to have a cult following—is a world overshadowed by depression, with crisis simmering under the surface until people revolt against the regulatory measures of an undemocratic government. It is a mirror image of the setting of news reports in the years following the outbreak of the global financial crisis in 2007 and of the 'Arab uprisings' that began late 2010, with revolts in these cases giving vent to outrage at the consequences of arguably just such a morality—of economic and political elites having acted in their own self interests. This chapter examines such news stories, told by journalists carrying the world in their broadcasts rather than on their shoulders, and whose philosophy is the professional one of objectivity, rather than Rand's (a)moral one of objectivism. The question in focus is how global crisis is dealt with in global newsrooms half a century after the first publication of *Atlas Shrugged*.

The three analyses that follow seek answers to this question in various ways, drawing on the concept of global crisis, as defined by Cottle (2009), and one that has been influential in recent scholarship on conflict reporting, media witnessing (Frosh & Pinchevsky 2009; Chouliaraki 2010b). In the first analysis, the notion of global crisis, expanded to incorporate the phenomenon of 'new wars' as defined by Kaldor (2003), is operationalised in a comparison of 844 headlines that topped broadcasts in 2011 and 2013 in BBCW, CNNI, AJE and RT. The second analysis explores the interaction between 'new' and 'old' media in coverage of the first weeks of the Arab uprising. It seeks to establish how global channels used, and represented the role of, social media in the turbulent events that threw changes in the media and political landscape into sharp relief. The third analysis focuses on discourse rather than technology, and considers attempts by BBCW and AJE journalists to make discursive connections between the people 'on the ground' (civilian and journalistic witnesses alike) and people experiencing events from afar (be they newsroom anchors or viewers in various parts of the world). This sort of discursive connectivity has a bearing on the relationship between the media and cosmopolitanism. Taken together, the results of the analyses suggest there is a need for critical reconsideration of scholarship that generalizes about how crises are depicted in global media, particularly claims that global conflict reporting has becoming 'Foxified' and reduced to 'infotainment' (Thussu 2009a: 113–132).

Global crises in global news headlines

Spilling across national borders and geographical territories, global crises, as defined by Cottle (2009: 2), include

> climate change and other human-induced ecological threats; the so-called 'war on terror' and new forms of militarism and warfare; world poverty, inequalities of international trade and financial meltdowns; looming energy crises, food insecurity and water shortages; as well as forced migrations and fast moving pandemics.

Disasters and extreme weather are on the list as well, together with struggles against human rights abuses throughout the world. In exercising their power, journalists can either do as the cosmopolitan optimists anticipate, and help the public understand that the crises they experience are shared, or as the political-economic sceptics assume, and by depicting the threats as distant play down the need for change. Cottle argues that global channels are key to the public definition of global crises, which are not just communicated by the media but also constituted by them, or 'mediatized'. The point Cottle is making is that how people collectively recognize and respond to threats on and to their interdependent planet are defined and enacted through the news media. Because the communicative structures through which contending views, voices and cultural values are disseminated and deliberated differ from one news culture to the next, global crises can be expected to be anything but homogenous. Little is known about this, however, as scholars have been 'empirically neglectful' of how global television news is structured, and how its mediating forms work (Cottle and Rai 2008c: 158). Given the tendency to become 'transfixed' on the 'live' quality of rolling news, there has been a failure to pay adequate attention to 'the repertoire of different communicative structures' involved, and to the different mediations that may result (Cottle & Rai 2008c: 161–2). Much closer attention should be paid, it is argued, to 'the play of views and voices accessed in traditional and emergent forms of international news correspondence' (Cottle & Rai 2008c: 163).

The exciting possibility that global crises are constitute within as well as communicated by the media is methodologically challenging, when it comes to empirical practice. The problem is how to distinguish issue (the denotative dimension of news reporting, or the 'communication' of crisis) from frame (the connotative dimension, on which crises are constituted within media reporting). It is relatively (although not entirely) unproblematic to code for 'issues' as being 'violent conflict', 'flood', 'unemployment' and so on. It is considerably more challenging to determine whether to code these as crises, because the decision to do so often depends on how the news story is told, not what it is 'about'. The latter raises methodological questions too. Is a violent conflict that claims 60,000–70,000 lives in a period of 20 months a crisis? Many people (scholars and journalists alike) would think of the civil war in Syria and answer in the affirmative. But what about a violent conflict, such as that which has dogged Israelis and Palestinians for decades? Such conflicts fit uneasily into the 'crisis' category, as the word has a double meaning. Apart from signifying a time of intense trouble or difficulty (as in most dictionary definitions), it also refers to a turning point or apex of such troubles. In this sense, a crisis is something reasonably finite.

There is, moreover, the question of who gets to decide whether that something is a crisis. A significant amount of research on crisis communication sidesteps the problem, by choosing an event (9/11, the tsunami or Hurricane Katrina) and then studying media reports of it. If the intention is, instead, to work from the empirical bottom up to the theoretical top, and to map out and systematise the incidence and types of crises that feature in news reports of different outlets, the task is less straightforward. Journalists seldom use the word 'crisis' when reporting on the sort of issues itemized by Cottle above (as will be shown in what follows). They occasionally use the word, or quote political actors who use it, to describe quite different problems. If a literal approach is adopted, 'a crisis of confidence' in the Church of England over the issue of gay (but celibate) bishops would be coded as a crisis, while devastating bushfires in Tasmania would not (because plucky Australians treat the firefighting as being 'all in a day's work' and evacuation and destruction of homes as 'a terrible shame but something you have to move on from').

The topics defined by Cottle as constituting global crises were used to structure a comparison of headlines in 233 broadcasts. Daily news programmes reaching European audiences mid-audience, broadcast by BBCW, CNNI, AJE and RT were coded for the months of January 2011 and January 2013.[37] The 844 headlines were coded as relating to global crisis if they referred to the war on terror/new war, economic crisis, climate change, other human-induced threat, disaster; energy crisis, forced migration, human rights abuse, food insecurity/water shortage, poverty or a pandemic. Kaldor's notion of 'new wars' (Kaldor 2003) captures the blurring of the distinction between war, organized crime and large-scale violations of human rights, including genocide, ethnic cleansing and terrorism. These were included in the coding criteria for the warfare referred to more generally in Cottle's definition. Although they date back to before Julius Caesar, 'assassinations' were coded as 'new warfare', as such acts tend to straddle the increasingly problematic boundary line between war, crime and terrorism. Not all the events in the material that were coded as crisis fit into this admittedly wide array of options, so under the category of 'other crisis', headlines were coded that related to protests that were violent or repressed with violence and other collective violence. Note was also made of when the word 'crisis' was actually used by the newsreader, even when not a crisis conforming to the 'global crisis' definition (a political crisis following a debatable election result in Côte d'Ivoire, for example). Finally, each headline was reviewed to determine whether it conformed to the 'global' adjective in the sense that it 'encompasses or moves across geographical terrains and political territories' (Cottle 2009: 2). This entailed coding a regional problem (such as the 'Eurozone crisis') as 'global', for present purposes.

What maps of a world in crisis are drawn by the four global newsrooms? The answer provided by the first, quantitative analysis indicates that there are problems with the homogenization thesis, and foreshadows the more general finding of the larger study reported in this book that the biggest differences are to be found, not between 'the West' and 'the Rest', but between the two 'counter-hegemonic' channels.

AJE shows the greatest degree of pluralism, when that is measured in terms of the geographical sweep of the top of its programmes: no fewer than 58 different countries featured in its headlines in the two months analysed here, as can be seen from Figure 3.1. CNNI mentioned the fewest, but due to technical problems, this can be reasonably attributed to the fact that fewer broadcasts were coded for that channel. There are as many RT as AJE broadcasts in the sample, however, and yet the Russian channel mentions only 36 different countries in the headlines. AJE and RT are also at different ends of the spectrum when it comes to the number of countries that feature in 'crisis' headlines—AJE mentions 44, which is twice as many as RT.

Figure 3.1. Number of different countries occurring in headlines of Al Jazeera English, BBC World, CNN International and Russia Today, January 2011 & January 2013 combined (233 broadcasts coded) and the number of countries occurring in 'crisis' headlines (figures in parentheses).

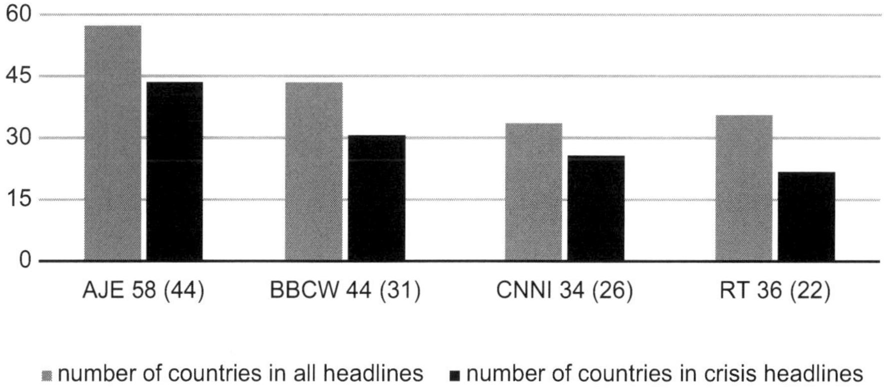

The differences become more noticeable when attention is turned to which countries feature most prominently in each channel. Table 3.1 shows the countries which occur most frequently in all headlines in the sample. Several things can be seen from this. First (as scholars such as Thussu and McPhail and journalists such as Rosenblum would have predicted), the United States tops the list. The only channel in which the US does not occur more often than any other country is RT, where Russia (at 25% of all headlines) dominates the news agenda. That said, the US features in more headlines in RT than it does in the other three channels, although CNNI comes a close second. The UK (18%) and France (15%) also feature largely in RT headlines, relative to the others (except for the incidence of the UK in BBCW, which weighs in at an unsurprising 31%). The prevalence of France will be returned to later, but for now the point to be made is that the countries dominating RT headlines are familiar from the East-West bifurcation in Cold War accounts of world politics.

The AJE map of a crisis-ridden world looks rather different. African countries occur in its headlines more often than in any of the other broadcasters. Were it not for the uprising in Egypt in 2011 and the French intervention in Mali in 2013, Africa would not even be on the RT map. Both BBW and CNNI gave prominence, in this period, to events in Tunisia and then Egypt, but caught on later to the significance of these developments later than AJE, so have a fraction as many headlines on them. AJE topped several broadcasts with the 2011 referendum in Sudan, while the others hardly mentioned it. The Anglo-Saxon channels were twice as interested in Australian floods and fires as they were in the mudslides that devastated Brazil; in AJE it was the other way around. (RT did not mention either.) In short, the 'South' is much more visible at the top of AJE broadcasts, even when aimed at prime-time European audiences, than it is in the other three channels. There are thus important differences between the two 'counter-hegemonic' channels. In contrast to the global gaze of AJE, the old East-West divide is apparent in RT headlines. It is also worth noting, given the refusal of the Russian government to sanction United Nations action to end the slaughter of civilians in the Syrian conflict, that country features in only 3% of RT headlines.

Table 3.1. Headlines in Al Jazeera English, BBC World, CNN International and Russia Today, January 2011 & January 2013 combined (233 broadcasts coded), distributed according to whether they are the sort of crisis referred to by Cottle (2009, 'Cottle heads'), other sorts of crisis (violent or violently repressed protests, political crises, other), and whether they can be considered 'global' ('encompass or move across geographical terrains and political territories').

Channel n= total # heads	'Cottle' heads	%	other crisis heads	%	all crisis heads	%	crisis named	%	global heads (crisis or not)	%
AJE both n=258	107	41.4	44	17	151	58.5	7	2.7	87	33.7
BBC both n=264	82	31	45	17	127	48	8	3	53	20
CNN both n=137	60	43.7	17	12.4	77	56	9	6.5	43	31.3
RT both n=185	62	33.5	13	7	75	40.5	1	0.5	70	37.8
Total n=844	311	36.8	119	14	430	50.9	25	2.9	253	30

Table 3.1 shows the distribution of 'crisis headlines' according to channel. Here again the two 'counter-hegemonics' are at opposite ends of the spectrum. More than half of the headlines in AJE (58.5%) and CNN (56%) have to do with crises. Almost half of BBCW's headlines relate to crisis, while for RT the figure is just over 40%. These figures reflect the relatively vigilant tone of AJE reporting. As the anchor quoted in Chapter 2 pointed out, AJE rarely smiles. Unlike the other channels, AJE broadcasts contain no ritual human interest or 'feel-good' items at the end, and the viewer who is interested in news of the British royal wedding (2011) or baby (2013), the Oscars, or French actor Depardieu's spectacular emigration to Russia would be well advised to choose one of its competitors. RT newsreaders, on the other hand, have a remarkably jocular mode of audience address. Almost all RT newscasts begin with headlines edged with cynicism, which newsreaders seem to find difficult to read without a sneer. CNNI's International Desk star anchor Hala Gorani begins most programmes with an urgent, energetic greeting that pulls viewers into her newsroom (although not usually into the field), and declares her

intention to get them straight to the top stories because 'we've got a lot to get through this hour'. This mode of address works to ascribe the viewer the role of the civic cosmopolitan, who feels obligated to inform themselves about the important events of the day.

'New wars' is a broad category, and one of the two months in the sample included both civil wars in Syria and Mali (the latter perhaps the more newsworthy due to French intervention) and a hostage crisis in Algeria, so it is not surprising that this crisis category tops the list for all four channels. Nor is it noteworthy that 'protests' come next, given that the first month in the sample saw the outbreak of the Arab uprisings. It is, however, worth observing the RT showed relatively little interest in those uprisings (3.7% of all RT headlines). Its top score of attention paid to human rights abuses are almost all due to reports on Guantanamo, and the continuing 'failure' of US President Obama to close the detention facility and release the prisoners being held without trial. Most of the human rights headlines in the other three channels have to do with violations perpetrated by the Syrian regime.

Table 3.2. Crises headlines in Al Jazeera English, BBC World, CNN International and Russia Today, January 2011 & January 2013 combined (233 broadcasts coded) distributed according to crisis category.

Crisis headlines	AJE	% AJE heads (258)	BBC	% BBC heads (264)	CNN	% CNN heads (137)	RT	% RT heads (185)	% All heads (844)
new wars/war on terror (n= 165)	60	23	41	15.5	30	22	34	18	19
violent(ly repressed) protests (n=76)	31	12	29	11	9	6.5	7	4	9
other political crisis (n= 40)	12	4.5	14	5	8	6.5	6	3	5
economic crisis (n= 38)	9	3	4	1.5	3	2	12	6	4.5
human rights abuse (n= 29)	10	4	7	2.5	1	0.5	11	6	3
disaster (n=16)	4	1.5	5	2	6	4	1	0.5	2
extreme weather event (n=39)	12	4.5	14	5	13	9	-	-	15
forced migration (n=10)	2	0.5	2	0.5	5	3.5	1	0.5	1

poverty (n= 8)	2	0.5	3	1	1	0.5	2	1	1
food/water insecurity (n= 7)	5	2	2	0.5	-	-	-		1
other human-induced threat (n=7)	3	1	3	1	-	-	1	0.5	1
climate change (n= 2)	-	-	2	0.5	-	-	-	-	0
other collective violence (n= 2)	1	0.3	1	0.3	-	-	-	-	0.3

The 'extreme weather' events that make their way into BBCW and CNNI headlines are Australian floods, heatwaves and bushfires, as well as snowstorms that paralyse the US and Europe. In AJE they are floods not only in Australia, but also in Brazil (which are accorded a significant amount of attention), Bangladesh and Mozambique.

The 'economic crisis' category features more prominently in the headlines of the 'counter-hegemonics' than in the channels based in countries suffering from the global crisis. RT pays more attention to the financial crisis, particularly in the Eurozone, than it does to the Arab uprising. Its framing of this will be explored in the next chapter. While southern Europe is generally thought to have been hardest hit, the woes of Greece and Spain pale into insignificancy while watching RT, where it is the UK that is depicted as experiencing the greatest problems. Russia, on the other hand, has no economic woes. Its only real crises are a ship stuck in the Arctic ice (a serial that topped several broadcasts) and the bombing of Moscow international airport (the work of Chechen terrorists, dealt with swiftly and forcefully by Putin).

The comparative analysis of the 844 headlines that topped the 233 news programmes broadcast by these four global news channels in the sample weeks show, in sum, interesting difference when it comes to how crisis is communicated and, in particular, how the world of crisis is constituted. The newsworlds are far from homogenous.

Reporting the Arab uprisings

As mentioned in Chapter 1, communication of crisis in recent years—and in particular of the popular uprisings against authoritarian regimes and their often violent repression—has put social media in the limelight. The second analysis addresses the problematic dichotomy often assumed to prevail between 'old' and 'new' media, focussing this time on the first weeks of the 'Arab uprisings'. Also referred to as the Jasmine Revolution, the Arab Spring or, by AJE, the 'Arab Awakening', this was a series of political revolutions that threw into sharp relief the impact of a parallel revolution in media technology.

The chapter's second analysis is based on the coding of 140 programmes broadcast over a period of nine weeks: from January 1st to January 31st 2011 and, as a follow-up study, AJE for the month of January 2012. Table 3.3 shows the distribution of material in the sample, which was extracted from 140 programmes containing 1862 items that took up a total of 4265 minutes, or 71 hours, of airtime.[38] Work began by watching of events as they unfolded—as the average viewer can be thought to have watched them—in the context of a given channel's overall news flow, followed by a closer reading of several weeks of broadcasts, one channel at a time, before coding basic features and entering them into a database. A note was made of each news item in which social media were used as a source of content (crowdsourced stills or video sequences, YouTube clips, tweets, etc.), whether or not this was expressly acknowledged, and the occasions on which social media were actually part of the story (in items about the 'Facebook Revolution' or the role of digital activism, for example).

Table 3.3. Distribution of material in the analysis of 'Arab uprising' reporting.

	# of programs coded	% of programs in sample	Length (in mins)	% total time	# of items	% total items
BBCW Jan 2011	31	22	774	18	395	21
CNNI Jan 2011	18	13	510	12	167	9
RT Jan 2011	31	22	635	15	211	11
AJE Jan 2011	31	22	1418	33	617	33
AJE Jan 2012	29	21	928	22	472	25
Total	140	100	4265	100	1862	99

CNNI and the Arab uprisings

Social media footage occurred in 11 International Desk items (of 167, i.e. 6.5% of all items). This was reasonably easy to ascertain, as CNNI clearly states the origin of material on the top right of the screen. Half of these items were about the uprising in Egypt.[39] Social media was the topic, or formed part of the narrative focus, in 7 items (4%), four of which were about the situation in Egypt, and one was about Twitter reactions to the 'revolution' (CNNI's quotation marks) in Tunisia.[40] Coverage of the Arab uprisings on this programme, in this period, was dominated by 'talking heads' and two-way lives, conforming to Thussu's view of global news formats. A number of items, and coverage on one day in particular, stand out however, and are worth considering more closely.

A piece on 25 January 2011 noted that social media were playing a 'big role' in fuelling the demonstrations in Egypt, as they had in Tunisia. The anchor showed two Facebook pages, described their purpose and contents, explained that Facebook had helped protesters coordinate, and reported that Twitter had been blocked. The evidence that the anchor, Hala Gorani, gives to back up such reports is worth noting:

> Based on some of the feedback I've gotten from people who follow me on Twitter and who follow developments in Egypt, it does appear as though some internet service providers have blocked Twitter in Egypt.

The following day, Gorani drew attention to new videos, which the CNNI team had been unable to confirm independently, of Cairo demonstrations:

> This is from our Facebook CNN fanpage, one of our viewers posting this new video. It gives you a sense really on the ground level of what's unfolding in the Egyptian capital.

On January 27th, the role of social media in organizing the protests again was the topic of a narrative of its own, with Gorani reminding viewers that 'the protests are being led by young, tech-savvy people who are using new social movement tools to organise themselves' before turning to Egyptian blogger Wael Abbas, on a telephone line from Cairo, for his thoughts. Abbas told her that what impressed him, when he went out on the street, was that it was not just filled with bloggers and activists: 'they are ordinary young people'. But Gorani pressed the blogger, urging him to agree that online activism had been important. Abbas complied, and said that social media had been a tool in organizing and sharing views and getting legal help: 'it's our media, the air we breathe in a country where they are trying to choke us'. Later, chatting to another talking head in the studio, Gorani noted that her interviewee was 'a young blogger, someone who spends a great deal of time online, who knows a thing or two about Twitter and Facebook and what it takes to get people organized'. She added that opposition leader Baradei was also reaching out through Twitter.

> so it's not just for young people. Politicians use it, activists use it, we as journalists—it's become a really important source of information for us.

CNNI journalists sat in the International Desk studio discussing what they were 'seeing online', and how people in Egypt were 'allowing their voices to be heard'. They observed that Twitter was being used to tell people how to get around the internet blockade, by tunnelling or proxies. Together, the CNNI journalists connected the audience outside Egypt to these activities, by noting that many viewers were contributing input from their own vantage points, submitting dozens of 'iReports'.

The following day's International Desk broadcast was different from the others. Gorani was joined in the studio by news veteran Jim Clancy, and together the two talked their way through the events unfolding live on January 28th. It was clear they had been sitting in the studio, broadcasting live for several hours, and they spoke to viewers as if they had been spent together, discussing live but blurry images of indiscernible people on nondescript streets that 'we' have 'all' been witnessing. Gorani joked that everyone had been 'playing the "where is Hosni Mubarak game" in the last two hours'. Social media were cast in a leading role in the unfolding drama, and Gorani used that media revolution to pull the audience into the action.

> In case viewers are wondering what's going on on the right side of the screen, this is the hashtag Egypt on Twitter. Look at this! This is something you rarely see, where every nano-second a new tweet on Egypt is registered on Twitter-dot-com. Inside of Egypt they may not have seen this because there is a near-total com shutdown [...] And by the way you can find us on Twitter at [...] We are continuously updating our viewers online and on the air on the situation in Egypt.

Having brought viewers into the event, CNNI was not going to let them go. On January 31st, after another interview with Abbas and an update on the battle to circumvent the information blockade, a reporter in the newsroom, who had been following Twitter trends, situated CNNI viewers as part of a global discursive event.

> You see people all over the world on every continent are tweeting and exchanging information and views about this [...] young and old on almost every continent are

very, very interested in exchanging views and sharing videos and comments about what is happening in Tahrir Square.

Two observations can be made on the basis of this reading of the CNNI material. The first is that social media themselves were being used relatively little, in January 2011 coverage of world events, compared to studio commentary (or 'talking heads'). But the other is that these media were being used in such a way as to make dialogic and discursive connections between viewers throughout the world, and people on the ground in Egypt.

BBC World and the Arab uprisings

The Arab uprising was extensively covered on BBC World during this period, which aired 65 items on it (16% of all BBCW news): 32 on Egypt, 24 on Tunisia, and one or two on Algeria, Yemen and the Sudan. Amateur video or still pictures were explicitly acknowledged as a source on only five occasions in this period, however.[41] Apart from agency material and excerpts from press conferences, a fair amount of footage seems to have been produced by the BBC's own cameramen, as there were several reporters deployed in the region during these weeks.

Social media were the topic of a story, or at least part of it, on four occasions.[42] Only two items related to events in Egypt. One of these mentioned, in passing, that protesters in Khartoum, inspired by the Egyptian revolution, had organized themselves on the internet. The final item, and really the only one that was about the role of social media in the uprisings, appeared towards the end of the January 28th programme. Even then, the main narrative was how the Egyptian authorities were attempting to control the internet, rather than the force for change that social media represented. But the reporter did note that

Protesters in Egypt and across the Arab world are mainly young and they have very powerful, peaceful weapons in their hands: cameras in their mobile phones. And the images flash around the internet, bringing others onto the streets.

One protester was interviewed as saying

Today every protester is a journalist uploading videos, pictures, straight from the field, from where the action is going, and taking place, with no censorship, it's all across Egypt. Traditional media can't compete with that.

Even if traditional media could not compete, the authorities could. After 're-markable pictures of defiance like this one got out', explained the reporter, referring to the iconic shot of a young man in front of an army truck equipped with a water cannon, 'the Egyptian regime has simply shut down modern communications, including mobile networks'. A graphic that showed the flow of internet traffic before and after the shutdown provided evidence of the assertion. No mention was made, as it had been on CNNI, of the ways activists used Twitter and proxy servers to bypass the internet blockade. Indeed, no mention of Twitter was made at all.

RT and the Arab uprisings

Social media feature in eleven RT items (of 211, i.e. 5% of all items). In only one of these was social media part of the story itself, and it was not about the Arab uprising. (It was about how Russian President Medvedev and former California governor Schwarzenegger used Twitter to agree on a ski date.) The other 'social media' items were all ones in which amateur footage occurred, together with other source material, although it was never actually attributed as a source. Three items using amateur footage were about unrest in Egypt and two about Tunisia.[43]

Unusually for RT, events in Egypt were the top story on January 28th. In this coverage, events in Egypt were placed in a global context. This contextualisation is a good illustration, it could be argued, of the notion of strategic narrative (Roselle et al. 2014). It provides a clue as to why so little use was made of social media in coverage of the uprisings, insofar as social media give voice to people on the streets who challenge unresponsive political elites.

> At least seven people have been killed in the turmoil, inspired by the month-long chaos in Tunisia where the uprising saw its leader deposed, 80 dead and a cabinet reshuffle. The images of angry protest in North Africa bear some striking parallels with elsewhere […] Georgia 2003, Ukraine 2004, Kirgistan 2005, Egypt 2011. Think these are all completely different revolts? Think again. […] If you look at the so-called people who are leading this, they are being coached by US intelligence services […] Ultimately, all aspirations come to nothing.[44]

AJE and the Arab uprisings

In January 2011, AJE mobilised a contingent of reporters to cover two events comprehensively—the referendum in Sudan, and the publication of the

Palestine Papers. But it was its coverage, first of events in Tunisia, and then in Egypt (and beyond the period in focus here), that ended up dwarfing that of its competitors, both in the number of items and the airtime devoted to the uprisings, and in the number of correspondents deployed on the ground. The AJE broadcasts coded here contain not less than 122 reports on the Arab Uprising, amounting to 20 percent of all AJE items that month. Of the 24 items using amateur footage as a source, 20 documented events in Tunisia and Egypt. While few of the items in the CNNI and BBCW broadcasts were actually about the role of social media, AJE explicitly focussed on its role in the uprisings in 12 items. It used—and acknowledged—footage taken from YouTube and other amateur sources, it incorporated tweets and citations from blogs in its narratives, and it highlighted the importance of Facebook and Twitter in several reports.

In one of these, broadcast on January 25th, the reporter explained that Egyptian activists had been inspired by events in Tunisia, and had been using the internet to call for a day of anger. 'For once', she said, 'it seems that internet clicks in Egypt have translated into action on the ground'. By the time that action had led to a political crisis and violent clampdown by security forces, another sort of digital technology began to feature largely in news reports. Google Earth was used to bring viewers from their armchairs down to the rooftops of the city in the throes of revolution. It took them to Tahrir Square with a live, exclusive feed that interrupted the programme on January 29th, and for much of the days that followed, AJE provided an open window on the square, and kept that window open even when there was little to see. It was not a matter of attracting viewers with arresting visuals or infotainment-spiced drama: it was simply a matter of being there.

In writing about global media coverage of 9/11, Grusin reflects on how the immediacy of televisual monitoring was combined with the hypermediacy of the web, and how the fascination of mainstream media with social media 'marked the transformation of the notion of perceptual or affective immediacy from the liveness of video to the connectivity of social networking'. But, he notes:

> With live video there is a sense of connection in real-time, with what is being shown on screen occurring at the same moment as you are watching it. With these Twitter feeds rushing past, however, there is a different temporality and a different affective sense. [...] what is being retweeted on cable news or on live blogs or other online sites has already happened in the past. It is not happening now. It is not immediate in the way that live video is. (Grusin 2010: 154)

While CNNI made much of Twitter, it was the unwavering gaze of the AJE camera on Tahrir Square that invited viewers throughout the world to attend the revolution.

Bearing witness

A substantial amount of work on the global public sphere is based on a Habermasian concern for deliberation in public. But Cottle and Rai suggest that it is not just reasoned debate and analysis that are vital to processes of political communication. Image and affect, experiential accounts and emotive testimonies also have a role to play (Cottle & Rai 2008c: 166).

As Scannell (2004: 582) reminds us, news structures and routines are designed to produce 'effects of truth', the purpose of which is to reassure us that we can believe what we are told and shown. Apart from live television feeds that open a window on revolutions as they take place, the consumption of first-person narratives is a way of 'being there'. Building on Boltanski, Scannell writes that all of those who are 'there' in different capacities, inhabiting different dimensions of spectatorship—be they participants, eyewitnesses, camera crews or reporters—act as witnesses to the truth of an event for the sake of absent audiences. 'They do this so that anyone and everyone who watches will "own" the experience (Scannell 2004: 582). In a typical crowd-sourced picture from a clampdown in one of the Arab uprisings, a participant protester holds up his foot as testimony to having physically witnessed the brutal response of the Libyan security forces. A second witness documents the experience with his mobile phone camera, an act witnessed in turn by a third, professional, cameraman. Because the moment was broadcast live, on global television, it produces a fourth dimension of witness—a viewer inhabiting Silverstone's mediapolis, participating in the moment in time if not space.

Frosh and Pinchevsky (2009) use the notion of media witnessing to denote 'the systematic and ongoing reporting of the experiences and realities of distant others' to mass (and in this case global) audiences. Like Peters (2009:24), they distinguish between three different dimensions, just as the image described above embodies different ones. Witnessing

> refers simultaneously to the appearance of witnesses in media reports, the possibility of media themselves bearing witness, and the positioning of media audiences as witnesses to depicted events.

The point of the distinction—and, conversely, the interweaving of the three manifestations into a single concept—is that it does justice to the complexity of mediated interactions. In some respects, the distant viewer owns the event more than the person on the ground. Spatial and temporal extension means that those who are not physically present are better informed about what is going on (they can see the 'big picture') than the people directly experiencing event, and perhaps even the reporter-spectator, whose account is reliant, for contextualization and sense-making, on the anchor in the studio, who conducts the choir of witnesses.

Just as the individual chorister is not the equal of the conductor, neither is the ordinary mobile phone-user the equal of a media professional. Not all crowdsourced footage will reach television audiences, and the journalist (or rather newsroom) is the guardian of the repeatability of events. (In other words, user-generated footage can be reproduced and recontextualized when the newsroom chooses, as pointed out by Lorenzo-Dus & Bryan 2011). Frosh and Pinchevsky (2009: 11) claim there is an institutional politics of contemporary media witnessing 'that informs how witnessed worlds are represented as shared and who may depict them and appear in them'. This assertion will be operationalised as a question to be posed, in what follows, to a smaller number of narratives of the events in Egypt. Two newsrooms are compared, one from each side of the mainstream divide—BBCW and AJE. In their stories of the uprisings, who is entrusted with the task of depicting the witnessed world of protest on each of these channels, who appears in this world, and how do they connect with us? Of particular interest are the narrative strategies which provide

> thick descriptions of reality by bearing witness and recovering something of the lived, experiential reality of news subjects and/or providing depth, background and analysis that purposefully seeks to move beyond the temporal/spatial delimitation of news event reporting (Cottle & Rai 2008c: 167).

The reading of the BBCW and AJE narratives paid particular attention to testimonies given by different sorts of witnesses, or on different levels of spectatorship. An answer was sought to the question: who tells us what is happening in these reports?

Table 3.4. Distribution of sources (people with speaking parts, counted once for every news item they speak in) in reports concerning the Arab uprisings on BBC World 9 pm CET and Al Jazeera English 8 pm CET, Monday 10 January–Sunday 30 January 2011.

	# men	% men	# women	% women	# vox pop/ activist	% vox pop/ activist	# elite	% elite
BBCW (n = 57)	47	82	10	17	32	56	19	33
AJE (n= 76)	58	76	18	24	40	52	29	38

Table 3.4 shows the answer to this question, i.e. the sources of testimony. In both BBCW and AJE coverage, the majority of those given voice are non-elites. They are activists, people who have taken to the streets to join the protesters or to witness the events themselves and in many cases to document the violence with which they were met, or people who have left their homes, the better to protect them. In BBCW reporting, those given a speaking part—activists and elites alike—are almost always men (82%). Men are in the majority in AJE too (76%), but there are differences between how the two broadcasters use sources that are worth noting. Half of the times a woman was coded as having a speaking part in BBCW, that woman was Hillary Clinton. On AJE, women are often pictured as leading the men into action and are often singled out in what in many cases appears to be a sea of young men. In one story, on January 25th, the (woman) reporter draws attention to how two women—one a young activist, the other an older housewife—both insist on being heard, taking their stance before the camera.

Unrest on the streets of Cairo is depicted by both channels as a crisis spilling across borders. But while BBCW correspondents readily tells a story of political elites (negotiating in Lebanon), the AJE journalists frame events in Lebanon as mirroring those in Tunisia. The narrative thus becomes centred on protesters taking to the streets to express their frustration over the government and their desire for change.[45] Witnessing is a key feature of this coverage. On January 26th, the AJE broadcast opened with an excerpt of an interview given over mobile phone by a young Egyptian woman, who finds herself in a crackdown by security forces as she was on the phone to Al Jazeera.

> And I'm trying to run now because they're targetting everyone, they're taking everyone, they're taking everyone and they're beating everyone and I'm running

> [inaudible] Oh my god, they're coming into the building, they're trying to take anyone who's running away. Sorry, excuse me, hello?

In Tunisia, AJE viewers had also been witness to disrupted testimony. On January 18th, the programme was co-anchored by a woman in London and another on the streets of Tunis, who presented a report filed by her male colleague in another part of the city. Viewers could watch the reporter talking, in English, to a youth on the street when police tried to stop the interview. The camera continued to roll as the AJE reporter reminded the policeman that his prime minister had declared freedom of the press. They stopped the conversation, said the reporter, but they can't stop the demonstrations. A young woman came up to him, and spoke directly to the camera, telling those witnessing the scene from afar that she had taken to the streets to fight for freedom and her country.

Another order of witness—already in evidence in the examples given above—is the reporter himself. Or herself, as was often the case in AJE, and as can be seen from Table 3.5.

Table 3.5. Number of items filed by a reporter (and not just read by the anchor) in BBC World 9 pm CET and Al Jazeera English 8 pm CET, Monday 10 January–Sunday 30 January 2011, distinguished by gender and whether they are on site.

	# items with reporter in the field	% items with reporter in the field	# of items with male reporter	% items with male reporter	# of items with female reporter	% items with female reporter
BBCW (n= 39)	25	64	32	82	7	18
AJE (n= 44)	40	91	28	63	16	36

Whatever the gender, it is worth noting the measures taken by these two broadcasters. In this respect, BBCW and AJE are different from CNNI and RT, who had far fewer reporters on the ground. By January 29th, the fifth 'Day of Rage', veteran correspondent Lyse Doucet was anchoring the BBCW broadcast from a Cairo rooftop. Departing from the usual programming ritual, an unusual quality is given to the liveness so often claimed to be an integral part of 24/7 news. Local Cairo time is repeatedly mentioned, as well as indicated on screen, and Doucet helps orient viewers in space as well as time, describing what she can see on the streets below. A reporter on the ground looks around as he talks, getting his bearings, and helping viewers to get theirs, describing the main square 'of the Arab world's biggest and most important capital' as 'a war zone'. A discursive connection is formed in such coverage between the people on the ground in Tunisia and Egypt (protesters and journalists alike) and the people witnessing events from afar (newsroom anchors and viewers around the world). Anchors in London and Doha continually ask their colleagues on stormy streets what they are witnessing. Sometimes the anchors see more than the correspondents—as for example on January 30th, when a few crowd-sourced pictures finally made it out of Alexandria, where there was a news blackout. Explaining that Al Jazeera's continuous coverage of the protests had prompted authorities to shut down the network's operations in Egypt, the anchor reminded audiences that correspondents were no longer being named, or their specific locations identified during live coverage, for their protection. In an exchange between the anchor and a correspondent on site (but not on camera) about the difficulty of getting pictures out because 'the lines of communication are being blocked at every corner, at every turn', the woman reporting from Alexandria replies

> It has been very difficult for anyone to broadcast anything out of the city. To begin with phones were shut down nationwide and after the phone network had returned internet still remains blocked [...] difficult for us to broadcast any material so these are very valuable pictures indeed [inaudible].

It was in these weeks that AJE became a household name, and saw its traffic surge by 2500%. Despite the difficulties in getting news out that its journalists testified to, it was this continuous, embedded coverage that led to Clinton's frustrated observation that Al Jazeera was winning the information war. It lost some important battles, however. The conviction that its reporters were too embedded—too sympathetic not just to pro-democracy protesters in general, but in particular to the Muslim Brotherhood that emerged victorious, the following year, in the first post-uprising elections—that led to the imprisonment in 2014 of three of its journalists, sentenced, as noted in Chapter 2, to seven and ten years for 'falsifying news' rather than bearing witness. The power struggle between news organizations and the military regime that subsequently wrested back power from the Egyptians on the street is not the point of the present discussion. Rather, it is that AJE coverage showed a new cohort of global viewers that it was different from other broadcasters. Throughout the weeks studied here, the world of AJE in particular was populated by people on the streets, rather than politicians in official buildings, who were largely conspicuous by their absence. Importantly, the streets were not just those of Tunis, Cairo, Manama and Benghazi—they were also those of European capitals, of Belarus, Albania, the Ukraine and Belgium, where people were depicted as calling for democratic reforms in their own countries. These were seldom anonymous, tending to be identified with names and roles (doctor, IT-engineer, art student or member of the youth movement). This study confirms the finding of Figenschou (2010), and the evidence of the journalists interviewed in Chapter 2, that the ambition is to give 'a voice to the voiceless'. In these weeks, it is alternative elites—notably young activists—who are interviewed in the AJE studio, rather than established figures. AJE coverage could be said to live up to its aspirations for diversity when assessed in terms of gender. While its loops of repeated raw video, just like the footage played and replayed in other global newsrooms and streamed online, showed largely masculine seas of protest, the reporters on site often managed to find a woman to interview. She may have been in jeans or in traditional Arab dress, but she often spoke English which, it could be argued, made it easier for non-Arab-speaking audiences to connect.

The metanarrative that can be discerned in AJE reporting in the period studied here was not one that flattered the besieged regimes in any region. The narrative was of resistance by young, peaceful, democratically inclined and globally oriented people 'on the ground' to corrupt, old men clinging to power that they had wielded for too long and misused, barricaded in their palatial residences not only in Tunisia, Egypt and Libya, but in Uganda, Côte d'Ivoire and Italy as well. These are narratives about, and recounted by, civil society. While BBC World paid considerable attention to the Arab Uprisings, and went so far as to co-anchor several programs from Cairo, its overarching narrative of the world emphasized instability and insecurity as opposed to change and hope, and it was told from an elite perspective rather than the vantage point of civil society. With the significant exception of Lyse Doucet's important roles in its narratives, the BBCW gaze is male, and the story of the uprisings is placed against a larger backdrop of a world populated by elites and powered by elite responses.

To wrap up

Shifts in the mediascape reverberate in the political realm on two dimensions. One is instrumental, and has to do with the role of media technology in dramatic, unfolding events—in seismic shifts like the uprisings documented here, which raze political fixtures and transform the political landscape in moments. The other is discursive. On this dimension, the scholar is challenged to make sense of processes that are less spectacular, and indeed not even particularly noticeable, but nevertheless likely to have a more enduring impact on society and politics. Just as climate change (not usually discernible) has more general and global significance than an earthquake (which can immediately be seen, heard and felt), the development of a sense of the world as a single place, to which the global circulation of media discourse contributes, could be thought to have farther-reaching consequences than a wave of uprisings.

Change on the second dimension is the more difficult to gain analytical purchase on, because the processes involved are less easily observed. Now and then, however, a door opens. The meta-narrative of 'the social media revolution' is one such point of entry, and it is instructive to reflect on how, in the weeks following the first anti-government demonstrations in Tunisia, both 'old' and 'new' media provided a portal on the crisis in the Arab world for people everywhere. The notion of connectivity is a helpful way of thinking about what was happening on both instrumental and discursive dimensions.

In future work on global crisis reporting, nevertheless, the analytical gaze should rest not just on the use of social media—which is not as essential to reporting as it is often made out to be—but also on the overall dramaturgy of rolling coverage, as Cottle and Rai (2008c) so rightly suggest—on the ritual of the news programme, and what happens when its routine is interrupted; on the role of the anchor in piecing together an account of turbulent events in dialogue with correspondents on the ground, who are in the thick of things but cut off in other ways: and on their relationship to other witnesses using a variety of new media forms. Like a liturgy with prescribed features (kyrie, sanctus, gloria, agnus dei), the news broadcast at normal times has a familiar tempo (top story, longer piece, telegram block, a bit about the Oscars or Royal Wedding at the end). In the first five weeks of the Arab Spring, AJE abandoned this ritual first, and more often than BBCW. By January 29th, however, BBCW had joined AJE in reporting directly from Cairo, and in giving saturation coverage to the revolution. The anchor remained the priest, through which all the voices were intermediated, but the form of the broadcast changed. Instead of the reporter playing the role of the first-order witness, telling viewers what was happening, global audiences could now see for themselves, and experience events as they unfolded, in real time. The vantage points were different—BBCW viewers joined Lyse Doucet on her rooftop, while AJE viewers looked straight into Tahrir Square—but all were urged to keep the company of the correspondents on site and stay tuned, for hours on end, even when nothing was happening and when no one could say how the unscripted event would end.

In an age when politics have become increasingly mediated (Thompson 1995; Couldry 2008) and perhaps even mediatized (Krotz 2009; Hjarvard 2008; Cottle 2009), the way in which news programmes frame protests, give voice to dissenters and implicate the people attending the demonstrations from their screen, co-present in time but not space, has a bearing on democracy, however conceived, and on broader theoretical debates about (cultural) globalization, discursive power and political change. The year that began with the uprisings in Tunisia and Egypt saw the world take to the streets. It was a time for outrage (Hessel 2011), and as such an instructive moment to analyze for the scholar seeking to grasp mediatization. The time for outrage has not passed. After the 2014 sentencing of Al Jazeera's Peter Greste, Mohamed Fahmy and Baher Mohamed, the BBC's Middle East editor, Jeremy Bowen, tweeted that 'Egyptian euphoria after Mubarak's fall feels a a world away'.

The 2011 uprisings spread to Syria, where the revolt evolved into a protracted conflict with staggering human costs and saw the rise of IS (Islamic State), whose actions sparked a global crisis par excellence. The challenges of covering the Syrian conflict have entailed considerable physical danger, spectacularly illustrated by the kidnapping and murder of journalists. They have faced other challenges in their work, about less dramatic aspects of the conflict. It is such challenges that comprise the focus of the rest of the book, which is about reporting not just conflict, but also cosmopolitanism. When interviewed for this study, one AJE correspondent, who is accustomed to reporting crisis and conflict, spoke about covering events in Syria and the work involved in explaining the perils facing refugees to viewers throughout the world. People assume it's always hot in the Middle East, she said, and didn't realize the refugees would be struggling with snow, a shortage of firewood and food. She found herself trying to 'penetrate' people's feelings of complacency and make them realize the Syrian refugee crisis is not a remote spectacle.

> It's not remote at all. These are people just like you, with problems that could be yours, and the implications of their problems may affect the price of food in your shops or the political decisions your parties take, or the alliances they make, or the arms they commit. [...] I've always felt, we're in this together, this planet is in this together, and whether it's climate change or major regional instability, whether it's starvation in one continent, or pollution in another, we're all going to suffer from

> this, if not now, later on. And it's to try to make people feel more involved as part of the global community, like you know, they might not look like you, but if you close your eyes, they'll sound exactly like you, their fears are your fears, and that's what I try to do with my broadcasting, to make people connect and care.[46]

The position expressed, with these words, is empirical evidence of what Berglez theorizes as global journalism, and what Cottle understands as global crisis reporting. It is an expression of an approach to reporting crisis that depicts the world as a whole, rather than as one of East-West divides, as in RT discourse. And it brings us to the perspective on global news to be discussed in the next chapter.

· 4 ·

BRAVE NEW WORLD

'O wonder!
How many goodly creatures are there here!
How beauteous mankind is!
O brave new world,
That has such people in't.'
Miranda's speech in *The Tempest*, Act V, Scene I, II

'whenever the masses seized political power,
then it was happiness rather than truth and beauty that mattered….
People still went on talking about truth and beauty
as though they were the sovereign goods.
Right up to the time of the Nine Years War.
That made them change their tune all right.
What's the point of truth or beauty
when anthrax bombs are popping all around you?
People were ready to have even their appetites controlled then.'
Aldous Huxley, *Brave New World* (1932/1994: 208).

Scholars who study global flows of people and ideas in terms of cosmopolitanism look at the evolving media landscape through a different ivory tower window than the writers in focus in Chapter 2, and see a space for fruitful encounters with different cultures and with people who are geographically and experientially distant. Scholars of mediated cosmopolitanism are interested in the narrative techniques that can bring the Other closer, or position the viewer by his or her side, or in his or her place. They are more likely to wear a happy face, as Hannerz (2004) put it, than the metaphorically furrowed brows of scholars critical of media globalization, and like Miranda in Shakespeare's *The Tempest*, draw attention to the beauty of the inhabitants of a 'brave new world'. Kind Miranda does not smile at everyone, however. She dislikes Caliban, the subhuman outsider who attempts to rape her, and chides him for his lack of education. The figure of this savage, forced into servitude to a vindictive aristocrat, has wandered through fiction, theatre and popular culture in the centuries since Shakespeare first drew him. In a reworking that has been central to postcolonial scholarship, Césaire turned Caliban into a black slave who revolts against his white master.

Huxley borrowed Shakespeare's phrase for the title of his dystopian novel of 1932. It depicts a future in which an 'ideal society' has been created by World Controllers (not the news corporations that control how people think and act in some accounts of media globalization reviewed in Chapter 2, but the rulers of a World State). Far from the vision of cosmopolitan theorists, this world society is populated by anonymous people who lead uniform existences under constant government surveillance. The hegemon controls their thoughts as well as behaviour, so they are duped into thinking they are happy. The exception is the outsider, John, who grows up in poverty on the Savage Reservation. Although an idealist, his life is miserable, and he retreats into the world of the imagination, with Shakespeare as his solace. Often said to be a critique of consumerism as well as political power, a central theme of Huxley's *Brave New World* is alienation. It is this, the antithesis of community, that explains why people behave the way they do.

This chapter looks through the thematic lenses provided by Shakespeare and Huxley at a selection of news reports that exemplify the narrative strategies of Russia Today and Al Jazeera English (and, to a lesser extent, BBCW). While these strategies differ significantly, it will be argued that the tropes of both versions of the 'brave new world' can be recognized in the news discourses of these two news channels, and that othering techniques can be seen at work in narratives that can be thought 'cosmopolitan' as well as in those that cannot. Depictions of space matter to this work, so particular attention will be paid to its use, both real and metaphorical. The ambiguous meaning and cynical inflection of the 'brave new world' image in Huxley's version can serve as a reminder that the people who work in global newsrooms can be understood either as complicit in the consumer-oriented processes that breed uniformity, or as storytellers who can encourage citizens to feel responsibility for people who are distant, defuse conflicts built on misunderstandings and lack of empathy for the plight of others, and raise an awareness of shared problems and futures.

Despite the ubiquity of global flows which bring people from different backgrounds into direct contact, simplistic depictions of Others persist and, indeed, thrive. Difference needs to be acknowledged and represented if cultural homogenization is to be resisted and something done about the increasing proclivity of Western societies to lower the national portcullis against migrants seeking refuge. But how is the journalist to report difference and represent societal diversity without tipping over into stereotyping? It is a constant challenge, admitted one of the respondents interviewed in this study,

> because news by its nature is simplifying things and kind of distilling them down to their core elements. The danger of that is of course that you sometimes do slip over into over-simplification and stereotyping. …That is a daily, hourly challenge, to avoid over-simplification, stereotyping'.[47]

As Resende and Paes (2011: 215) have argued, rather than asking whether media narratives make it possible to get to know the Other, 'the question to be raised in this landscape has more to do with how media builds—or helps intertwine—the contact between the I and the Other'. Given that meaning is always both absent and present, and can only be grasped when located in discourse and read in context, another purpose of this chapter is to illustrate, once more, the importance of comparative research. It begins with a brief consideration of the problem of representation as addressed in film, cultural and media studies before going on to review ideas of relevance to the notion of cosmopolitan space. Different versions of space are then mapped in news reports broadcast by RT and AJE in the weeks before elections to the European Parliament in 2014 saw a surge in support for anti-immigration parties. It will be argued that while RT 'others' the US and UK in its reports of May 2014, drawing a discursive map familiar from the Cold War, AJE's narrative technique is provocative rather than propagandistic. The narrative strategies used by AJE journalists to reverse the gaze, and their forays into the liminal space of the margins, means they find—and show—the 'global south' in both Europe and the US.

The problem of representation

In a classic essay, Dyer (1977) distinguishes between 'typing' and 'stereotyping'. A type, in this account, is a characterization that foregrounds a few widely-recognizable traits. Everything about a person or culture is reduced to those few features by the stereotype, which depicts them as enduring and natural. A symbolic border guard, the stereotype maintains order—both social and symbolic—by weaving 'Us' into an imagined community and exiling those who are different to stay, like Caliban and John Savage, 'beyond the pale'. An instance of the struggle for hegemony, stereotyping is a discursive power game that involves the application of the norms of one's own culture to those of others, and seeing the world through one's own eyes rather than those of the sophisticated viewer (Boulding 1959; Robertson 2010).

It is difficult to find a scholar who has provided a more insightful and pedagogical account of the relationship between media representation, stereotyping and othering in global settings than Hall. Central to his account is the idea that culture has to do with shared meanings, and depends on the members of a given culture viewing what is happening in the world around them in similar ways. Meaning comes from how things are represented, 'the words we use about them, the stories we tell about them, the images of them we produce [...] the ways we classify and conceptualize them' (Hall 2007: 3). This matters to news accounts of the world beyond the borders of the nation because such representations contribute to an understanding of where and with whom we belong. Global communication has the potential to destabilize such meanings, which circulate between different cultures 'on a scale and with a speed hitherto unknown in history' (ibid.).

'Otherness' has been approached by scholars from a variety of disciplines in a variety of ways. Following Saussure, linguists argue that meaning could not exist without difference. We can only conceive of something by contrasting it with something which it is not: white is 'not-black'; British is 'not-African'. Theorists of language who have been inspired by Bakhtin argue that what it means to be Canadian or Scandinavian or European is 'always up for grabs, always being negotiated' in a dialogue between cultures and their 'others'. Anthropologists see culture as depending on things being consigned to different categories and to different positions in systems of classification, and on them becoming imbued with meaning in such structures. When things find their way to the wrong category or 'get out of place', as it has been put, the order is disturbed. People who 'belong' try to restore order and clean up the communal space (Hall 2007: 234–6).The result, it is argued, is racist reactions to immigrants and other foreigners, or members of marginalized religious or ethnic groups. The growing influence of anti-immigration parties throughout Europe and elsewhere ensures the continuing relevance of such theoretical perspectives, and the appropriateness of a metaphorical frown.

Other trends are also in evidence, however—both theoretical and imaginative. As mentioned, cosmopolitans are more likely to wear a smile, and what Ong (2009: 450) has called 'the common thread' that ties together the many versions of cosmopolitanism is the inclination to welcome and engage with the stranger. Rather than being tidied away, the Other is brought closer using a variety of imaginative strategies. A key concept here is Arendt's 'proper distance', which, it will be recalled, was reworked by Silverstone (2007). He used the notion to think about the

> degree of proximity required in our mediated interrelationships if we are to create and sustain a sense of the other sufficient not just for reciprocity but for a duty of care, obligation and responsibility, as well as understanding. Proper distance preserves the other through difference as well as through shared identity (Silverstone 2007: 47).

Cosmopolitanism is increasingly seen as having a moral dimension (Chernilo 2012; Delanty 2012; Mendieta 2012; Papastergiadis 2012; Strydom 2012; Vernon 2012), not least in the literature addressing its mediated preconditions (Chouliaraki 2006, 2008, 2010a and 2010b, 2013; Dencik 2013; Silverstone 2007; Stevenson 2003; Orgad 2012). This mediated morality is closely related to cosmopolitanism's search for contrasts (Ong 2009: 458). By working on the imagination, news narratives can provide semiotic resources to nourish the cosmopolitan imagination, and help form discursive connections with distant others—whether they are toppling regimes, as in Chapter 3, or pursuing mundane existences—by showing that they may not be distant after all.

But narratives and the storytelling techniques that shape them can also literally put screens before the eyes of the viewer; they can make the world smaller (which is not the same as making it more intimate) and limit the imagination by imposing order on a chaotic world. Seen this way, narrative limits hybridity or, as Bauman (1991) would have it, ambivalence, i.e. the possibility of things being assigned to more than one category. Orgad, who builds on this insight, argues that this 'morally suppressive force of narrative' is 'extremely pronounced' in mediated accounts of the global financial crisis (Orgad 2012: 197). That narrative is said to be one of failing global structures and 'incoherence' in the workings of the 'hegemonic rationality' (Couldry 2010), with little seen or heard 'of the consequences of economic restructuring for families and the costs that individuals incur in order to enter and stay in the market'. The 'dominant narrative of the market' continues to be reproduced, and the societies of the European South are 'infantilized and ridiculed' in news reports (Orgad op. cit.).

How the dominance of a given narrative is established empirically is not clear, and a leitmotif of this book is that it is unhelpful to generalize about news reports: what happens in them is a matter for empirical analysis, preferably comparative. Interviews with journalists working for one of the global newsrooms that features here certainly provide evidence of quite different ambitions than ridiculing the South. As one journalists put it, the aim is to show how people—wherever they are—are affected, 'whether it's a financial crisis, an immigration crisis, any kind of crisis'.[48] The South, to these journalists, is not some fixed, essentialized entity. Another journalist explained that at AJE,

> we report the South, so we report the European South. Which doesn't mean Greece, but the south in Sweden. We give a voice to the voiceless and the voiceless in Sweden, who they are, we go to them.[49]

The 'South', in these narratives of the newsroom, emerges as a discursive construct (like gender or race) as much as a geographical site. Giving a voice to the voiceless is accomplished, as reported in Chapter 2, by telling the 'high helicopter' story of the state of the British economy through the eyes of the individual, or the story of the Greek crisis from the perspective of 'a baker on Thessaloniki or in Corfu who is struggling to make ends meet', as one journalist put it.[50] Another narrative strategy is to show viewers that global problems can reverse the human, economic and communicative movements often assumed to flow from the West to the Rest. The challenging of stereotypes itself can make for good news, according to another respondent, who illustrated the point with reference to a story about Germans going to Turkey to find work, instead of the other way around.[51]

How these ambitions are effected in practice will be explored shortly. Before that, however, the idea of reporting the South brings the chapter to a consideration of the scholarly literature on communicative geography.

Space, place and news maps

Hallin has observed that journalists do more than inform people about where an event takes place: 'they also tell us where we are in a more general and much more important sense' (Hallin 1986: 110). While they may focus on the specific, 'grander images' of the world emerge implicitly in the news, delineating territories of 'Freedom' and 'Totalitarianism', for example. Space, he opined, is part of a world image that was experiencing a renaissance in the mid-1980s: that of the 'cold war battlefield'. Three decades later, tensions between Russian and Western leaders over Russia's annexation of the Crimean peninsula in March 2014 and the subsequent seizure by separatists of parts of eastern Ukraine, together with revelations of the surveillance activities of US and British governments, have ensured that the cold war imagery has not lost currency.

Hallin argued that 'place' has five functions in news reports. It can bolster journalistic authority, by assuring news consumers that the reporter was there and is thus well-informed. It can provide social connection when, for example, the hometown of the foreign minister is mentioned in reports of her visit to a foreign country. Place serves the function of 'subject' in news reports chronicling, for example, attempts to save Venice from rising water levels (to transpose Hallin's older, and US-centric idea on contemporary global concerns). Finally, place can serve as setting. It is this fifth function that is of most relevance to the present discussion. Hallin notes that most news stories actually lack settings, because so much news is about policy, and thus 'takes place' at the non-site of the press conference, but also because setting is a powerful rhetorical device. When a news story begins with a place, it is no longer 'objective': the reader, listener or viewer is invited to experience the event or issue, and not just be informed about it. Because of the discursive power involved, setting is rarely used in political reporting, according to Hallin. Journalists instead keep to the 'dispassionate' reporting style that is considered to be appropriate to hard news (1986: 125–6). But this style of reporting is inadequate to a complex world, in Hallin's view, because it is too abstract. At the same time, he enjoins journalists to take more responsibility for 'the general images of the world they convey' because they are not simply reporters. 'They are teachers, preachers, and ideologists: they tell us how to see and understand the world' (1986: 145).

While Hallin's reflections appeared in an anthology under the theoretically neutral heading of 'where' (operationalising one of the traditional 'who, what, where, when, why' questions), Adams & Jansson (2012), think in more abstract terms, and differentiate between 'space' and 'place'. Space implies movement—of people, goods, capital and communication—both actual and potential. Spaces can be understood as 'structured systems of connectivity' and structures of opportunity and expectation (2012: 312). Places, on the other hand, 'are both material and symbolic' and relate to 'deeply layered subjective experience' grounded in local experience (2012: 301, 307). Similarly, Gutsche draws on Harvey to conceive of space as having to do with the identification and marking of a particular geography for a specific purpose, and 'place' to refer 'to the meanings assigned to a geography or location that has been recognized as a particular space' (Gutsche 2014: 492).[52]

There is a long-standing and interdisciplinary interest in the relationship between maps and storytelling. Filmmakers have used maps extensively, to locate and ground their narratives and 'to stimulate the imagination of their audiences', notes Caquard (2011: 2), who draws attention to technologies and discourses that contribute to the discursive construction of intermediary spaces between real and fantasy worlds (2011: 6). In this imaginative sense, news media draw maps that connect the local to the larger world, suggests Gutsche (2014: 488), 'by presenting local news through larger, cultural narratives of and about people and places'. In contrast to the satellite images on base maps with which Google users have become familiar, and which connected distant viewers to the place of real-time revolution in Chapter 3, the place-making in evidence in the atlases that have adorned schoolroom bookshelves for centuries contain relative and socially constructed places such as North, South, East and West, Orient and Occident. In their reports, journalists reproduce the ideological and cultural messages embedded in such representations, understood as cultural sites 'where meanings are constructed, shared and reconstructed' on a daily basis (Gutsche 2014: 492–3).

A recurrent concept in this scholarly discourse is that of a 'third' space. The idea is attributed to Bhabha (2004), who was concerned with the 'unequal and uneven forces of cultural representation' (2004: 245), and invokes the space of the margins, where the oppressed talk about how to become free, or the space where oppressor and oppressed come together. Like Caliban, the idea of third space has been appropriated and reworked by scholars, writers and artists in a variety of contexts. It is generally used to designate a hybrid space in which people, who do not share a geography, can come together and relate to each other, and has inspired scholarship that explores 'how news media assign meanings to environment through narratives of space' (Gutsche 2014: 487).

The contributors to an anthology on 'cosmopolitan geographies' (Dharwadker 2001) share a scepticism of the scholarly proclivity to treat cosmopolitanism 'in a dehistoricized or delocalized "ideological space"' because cosmopolitanism should not be understood as something abstract, but rather an orientation on the world grounded in time, space and culture (Dharwadker 2001: 2). What is useful about exploring theoretical notions of otherness, space, place and cosmopolitanism through the empirical analysis of news narratives is that this focus makes it possible not just to access the third space and imaginative realm, but also to explore depictions of real places and flows between them.

The space of Europe

Daily reports broadcast over a six-week period, from 1 May to 11 June 2014, by AJE and RT were analysed and compared with those of BBCW to see whether different versions of Europe emerge. In the background of the European election campaign that took place in these weeks, boatloads of Northern African migrants floundered in the attempt to reach Europe, and French police razed camps of asylum-seekers. The period also saw the 10th anniversary of former Warsaw Pact states joining the EU, the 100-day mark in the run-up to the Scottish referendum on independence, and the commemoration of the 70th anniversary of D-Day, which previous research (Robertson 2010) has shown provides a powerful narrative frame for reflections on the European journey from conflict to cosmopolitanism. The period was also marked by tensions between Russia and Europe over the Ukraine.

Table 4.1 juxtaposes the topics of 'Europe' reports, ranked according to frequency, to make it easier to compare the different priorities of BBCW, AJE and RT. It shows that, while there are some similarities when it comes to which events or problems are covered, the three global broadcasters depict quite different Europes. The European Parliament elections notwithstanding, the Europe of BBCW is characterised by politics played out within national settings. The 'migration/refugee' category of Table 4.1 is dominated by two British events: the controversy surrounding the possibility that Muslim militants had integrated a Birmingham school, and the release of figures showing that the UK had not been inundated, as expected, by Romanian and Bulgarian migrants when the border was opened to them at the turn of the year. In keeping with other reporting, BBCW pays considerable attention to past events, and makes space for culture and human interest stories.

Table 4.1. Hierarchy of issues in reports of Europe, 1 minute or more in length, broadcast on BBC World News, Al Jazeera English and Russia Today, 1 May–11 June 2014.

BBC World n=73	Al Jazeera English n=49	Russia Today n=54
domestic politics, 12 (16%)	disaster, accident, 11 (22%)	international relations 9 (16.6%)
EU politics & election, 11 (15%)	migration, refugees, 9 (18%)	military issues, 6 (11%)
migration, refugees, 8 (11%)	EU politics & election, 5 (10%)	EU politics/election, 6 (11%)
culture, 7 (9.5%)	domestic politics, 5 (10%)	protest, 6 (11%)
disaster, accident, 6 (8%)	culture, 4 (5%)	domestic politics, 6 (11%)
commemoration, 6 (8%)	economy/crisis, 2 (4%)	right-wing extremism, 5 (9%)
scandal, 5 (7%)	international relations, 2 (4%)	economic crisis, 3 (5.5%)
crime & corruption, 5 (7%)	social problems, 2 (4%)	social problems, 3 (5.5%)
protest, 3 (4%)	protest, 2 (4%)	energy, 3 (5.5%)
human interest, 3 (4%)	commemoration, 2 (4%)	migration, integration, 2 (3.7%)
hate crime, 2 (3%)	hate crime, 1 (2%)	culture, 1 (1.8%)
economics, 1 (1%)	other, 4 (5%)	commemoration, 1 (1.8%)
other, 3 (4%)		hate crime, 1 (1.8%)
		other, 2 (3.7%)

In Europe reports in AJE in this period, disaster tops the list. Behind this finding lie the floods in the Balkans, to which the channel devoted far greater resources than the other two. This category is closely followed by migration and refugees, which account for 18% of all its Europe reports, followed by elections to the European parliament. RT covers issues that neither of the others mention, and draws attention to military topics (such as NATO exercises in the Baltic and UK arms sales to authoritarian regimes throughout the world) not covered by the others. International relations top the RT hierarchy of issues in Table 4.1, reflecting attention paid to diplomatic tensions between the EU and Russia over the Crimea and Ukraine, and Germany's quarrel with the US over the latter's spying. Migration comes relatively low down on the list, while the problems of Europe come higher up—protests, extremism and social and economic crisis.

Table 4.2. The space of Europe: countries comprising Europe, and the nationalities of people speaking in reports of Europe, 1 minute or more in length, broadcast on BBC World News, Al Jazeera English and Russia Today, 1 May–11 June 2014. The numbers indicate the number of items in which the country features or a person of a given nationality speaks. ('EU' is counted as a country for the purposes of comparison.)

BBC World n=90 country-mentions, 23 countries	Al Jazeera English n=65 country-mentions, 14 countries	Russia Today n=63 country-mentions, 19 countries
UK, 23 (25.5%)	UK, 11 (17%)	UK, 18 (28.5%)
France, 10 (11%)	Serbia, 11 (17%)	EU, 12 (19%)
EU, 8 (8.8%)	Bosnia, 8 (12%)	Germany, 7 (11%)
Turkey & Spain, 6 (6.6%) each	France, 7 (10.7%)	Greece, 6 (9.5%)
Germany, Ireland, Italy, 4 (4.4%) each	EU, 6 (9%)	Spain, 4 (6%)
Greece, Bosnia, 3 (3.3%) each	Turkey, 5 (7.6%)	Poland, Estonia, 2 (3%)
Portugal, Poland, Denmark, Serbia, Belgium, Austria, 2 (2%) each	Greece, Spain, 4 (6%)	Denmark, Italy, Switzerland, Belgium, Sweden, France, Portugal, Czech Republic, Hungary, Romania, Bulgaria, Turkey, 1 each (1.5%)
Romania, Bulgaria, Croatia, Holland, Monaco, Switzerland, the Vatican, 1 (1%) each	Italy, 3 (4.6%)	
	Portugal, 2 (3%)	
	Belgium, Germany, Ireland, Monaco, 1 each (1.5%)	

Seen in terms of the countries that comprise the space of Europe in the reports of the three newsrooms, and the nationalities of the people who speak in them, there are again differences worth noting, as can be seen from Table 4.2. The emphasis is on western Europe in BBCW and on the south in AJE, while the Europe of RT is comprised of former Warsaw Pact countries that do not figure in the Europes of the other. Those who chose to join the EU bitterly regret their decision, in RT accounts. There is a higher proportion of reports about the UK in RT than in BBCW (28.5% and 23%, respectively) and considerably more than in AJE (17%). That is not to say that it is the same UK in all versions. In BBCW it is, naturally, 'us', while in RT, it is clearly 'them', as will be seen below.

The space of Europe in BBCW

BBCW's reporting of the EU elections emphasizes European divisions—between East and West, old and new, left and right, political elites and the disinterested public. Two reports in this period can be mentioned for their interesting use of space.

In an item broadcast on 1 May 2014, for example, it tells 'a tale of two Europes'. Some parts of Europe were celebrating a decade of EU membership that day, began the newsreader, not least 'eight former communist countries for whom it was a return home to the European economic family'. The 'first' Europe of the report—Portugal—was described as 'elegant, beautiful and old', but the BBCW journalist notes that even its employed are suffering. 'Whereas Poland', says the correspondent in Warsaw, catching the EU flag that his colleague in Lisbon had thrown down on the cobblestones, 'still feels like a place on the up'. Poland, it is explained, has been modernized by tens of billions of euros in development aid, deployed in the huge rural economy. But a huge number of Poles still have to look for work abroad, and free movement within the EU has been a lifeline.

In a follow-up story, the BBCW anchor asks how much the EU affects 'our' daily lives, and the Brussels correspondent comes back to England to find out (despite the fact that many BBC World viewers do not live their lives in Britain). The reporter goes to a 'typical' English city, and a 'typical' restaurant on the High Street, and orders a 'typical' British 'fry-up'. Sitting in front of a serving of fried eggs, fried bacon and sausage and fried bread, the reporter explains to viewers

> basically everything you see on this plate is affected by EU rules. For instance, the way the pigs that produce the bacon are reared, the meat content in the sausage, the PCBs in the pesticides in the crops used to grow the crops in the first place, in fact EU legislation also regulates how many hours the people who pick the vegetables can actually work out in the fields. But quite often British standards are higher than Brussels standards…

Europe, in this narrative, comes to Britain, where it controls and homogenizes as in Huxley's world state. But the piece is also an example of what Berglez calls for in his domesticating version of global journalism. Either way, the space of the narrative is British, and regulated from without.

The space of Europe in AJE

The Europe of AJE, by way of contrast, is not overly regulated, and instead of juxtaposed to Britain is connected to larger global flows.

> There's a long tradition of economic migration from Europe's former colonies by those seeking work in the former colonial power. The financial crisis is now forcing some Europeans to make the journey in reverse

says the newsreader in one report about economic migration, her words echoed by a reporter in Lisbon who pulls viewers into 'a world turned upside down'. A Portuguese restaurant owner explains why he is selling up and leaving for Mozambique, where he hopes to open a hotel, and a Portuguese lawyer talks about emigrating to Brazil which, he says, is 'booming'. The camera rests on statues of explorers looking across the water which, explains the newsreader, celebrates the Portuguese heroes from the age of discovery,

> the men who set out across the world, conquering new territories and building a vast empire. Today, in a strange way, history has come full circle, as the Portuguese head back to the former colonies looking for work.

Centre and periphery feature in other AJE stories of Europe as well, and space is a central narrative device in a story broadcast on 16 May 2014. It too begins in Lisbon, but in this case it represents the space of the European centre, and the live debate between candidates for the European presidency, who speak to a large hall and to the cameras broadcasting the debate on television and streaming it on the internet. The setting then shifts to London, and the reporter standing by the River Thames, with the British parliament buildings in the background. He explains that while the European presidency is both an important and controversial post, 'it barely made a blip on the news agenda', and asks Europeans what they think. A map takes him to Portugal, and a space in it opens to reveal a man in a motorcycle helmet on a Lisbon street. He says he cares who the next European Commission president is, but not enough to watch the debate. The map swerves and the camera zooms in on Athens, and another window opens on a man standing beside an automatic teller. He says he didn't watch the debate because European politics are corrupt, but correctly identifies the current president by name. The ground shifts again and a young man appears in the map of France. He expresses interest in local and national politics, but not European politics. Winding up, the reporter opines that the main rival of the contenders for the European presidency seem to be apathy and cynicism. The space of the European centre is depicted, in this narrative, as aloof and disconnected from place, and from the localities of the ordinary European.

The space of Europe in RT

All is not well in the Europe depicted by RT. Corporate profits and the intent of governments to balance budgets is valued over the well-being of ordinary people; social injustice is rife. The EU is not 'uneasy', as in AJE, or 'divided' as in BBCW discourse: in RT, it is 'traumatized'.

> In 2004, the EU undertook its biggest single enlargement, absorbing a vast area of the continent's East. The going since, though, has been tough, with austerity, recession and unemployment all playing their parts. So was it all worth it? ('Take-in Trauma', RT, 4 May 2014)

Another report explains that austerity and suicide now go hand-in-hand in Greece, as 'a study directly links most suicides in 2009 and 2010 to the budget cuts'. From having had the lowest rate in Europe, the number of suicides spiralled to a 'huge number' with the recession that plagues the West. Neither the authors nor the title of the study documenting this are given, nor any information about the research involved, but people on the streets of Athens are asked to give their views on its results ('Driven to Edge', 5 May 2014). This is a typical RT narrative technique, deployed together with phrases like 'an opinion you often hear in the Czech Republic', without specifying or backing up what remain essentially hearsay (4 May 2014).

The annual Mayday rallies are 'marred by violence' as people take to the streets of Istanbul, Athens, Berlin and London, 'fed up and desperate'. (By way of contrast, the Mayday demonstrations in Moscow involve 'festivities' enjoyed by over 100 thousand people.) Supporters of the whistle-blowing movement in the UK hand over a petition to 10 Downing St, 'demanding protection for those who shed light on government and corporate wrongdoing' instead of having 'the door slammed in their face' (May 1st). In an item broadcast on May 3rd, entitled *Money vs Medicine*, viewers are told that barely a week goes by without a story about the impact government cuts are having on the National Health Service, and that paramedics are now speaking out (although none are identified by name in these reports). A few days later, a newsreader (by now sporting the St. George ribbon banned that week by the Ukrainian parliament) tells viewers something they would not learn from either BBCW or AJE.

> The UK likes to pride itself on being a defender of human rights, but when it comes to making money, it can seem to forget its principles. Last year, Britain signed arms contracts worth billions of pounds with countries that its government now admits have poor rights records and harbour extremists...

Back in the UK, a 'new poll' shows that a third of the people fear the spread of android technology, should killer machines end up in the hands of the military ('Paranoid Android', 12 May 2014). When other media, including BBCW and AJE, were reporting the trial, in the Hague, of Ratko Mladic, the Serb military commander in the Bosnian war accused of 'the worst crimes against humanity that Europe has witnessed since the Second World War' (*The Guardian*, 16 May), RT chose instead to air two pieces on British war crimes instead, committed in Iraq. The British are depicted in RT as obese (6 June), cruel to the homeless (10 June), and intolerant.

> The principle of tolerance is held so highly in the West that some there say they're now afraid to express their views freely for fear of a witch-hunt. Use the wrong word, and you could end up being labelled as something nasty. RT looks at whether freedom of speech is being eroded by an obsession with political correctness. ('Shut-Up Culture', 16 May 2014)

'Racist, homophobic, xenophobic': this report opens to a list of epithets as the pop refrain 'shut up, just shut up, shut up' is played in the background. From MPs to the average guy on Twitter, people with views that go against the mainstream are shut down with 'faux moral outrage', viewers are told. Although they took place a decade before the programme was broadcast, the examples cited (the murder of Theo van Gogh and death threats on the life of Ayaan Hirsi Ali, who renounced her Islamic faith) are reported as if they are fresh. The primary defines, in this work of othering the UK, are people like the CEO of Mozilla, who claims that he had to resign over his support for anti-gay-marriage legislation. The chairman of Liberty GB, a racist, is cast in the role of the victim of a political arrest. The RT reporter observes:

> When political arrests happen elsewhere, Britain often loudly takes a stand. Here, though, the response has been worryingly muted.

Just stories

The theme of injustice is an important one in RT discourse, and a key dimension of the othering techniques deployed by its journalists. These can be compared to two quite different narratives of justice to be found in the AJE sample, which make strikingly different use of space and othering.

Wasted lives

In RT, the perspective throughout is that of the innocent victim of economic injustice. Joining the euro is bad news for Estonians: 'while officials celebrate, Estonians fear the single currency will make their poor living standards even worse'. In the UK, 'public fury is growing' as banks, bailed out by taxpayers' money, prepare to hand out a bonanza of bonuses.

> This is austerity Britain. The homeless and needy queue up for food handouts from charities all over London and the UK. But just a few miles away, it's a different world with different rules.

The RT perspective, and use of actor perspectives to frame economic crisis reports, is typified by an item following the US President's State of the Union address: 'if, as Obama said, we measure progress by the success of ordinary people, then there's little ground for optimism'. In the RT discourse, the ordinary people will always lose out, because the system is structured so as to pit 'fat cats' against overburdened taxpayers and to ensure that the richer get richer while the poor get poorer. The world outside Russia is depicted as one of growing social and economic inequality. It is not always the fault of the establishment, however. Americans, for example, have themselves to blame as well, as they are 'shopaholics', 'addicted to consumerism' (although some have had enough, and have started reading Marx and performing acts of economic disobedience).

Recurrent RT reports link suicide to austerity policies. 'A study' (the authors and title of which are not given) is the hook for a story broadcast on 5 May 2014 that links most suicides in Greece in 2009 and 2010 to budget cuts, with almost one person a day taking their lives in that period. The reporter goes to Athens to speak to men who have been driven 'close to the edge'. A man identified as Pavlos, unemployed and homeless, says it is hard to get a job. 'They prefer to use migrants who are cheaper and don't ask for any benefits'. It is a brief conversation: the people with speaking parts are passersby, a man who almost took his life, and a psychologist who sees a direct link between the Greek crash and soaring suicides. A well-dressed young woman who stops to talk to the reporter says she has been unemployed for two years and while she still has to pay for everything, understands why it is mostly men who commit suicide: 'they have more responsibility'. The camera rests, at the end, on a man who has passed out on the ground in front of his wheelchair, his head on his knees and the scars on his bare legs visible. People don't really want to die, says the psychologist: people want to kill their pain. The problem is, concludes the reporter, there remains a lot of pain in Greece after six years of austerity, and very few signs of hope to cling to.

Piles of waste comprise a recurrent image in the RT discourse. Financial recession is linked to moral recession and an excess of refuse lining the streets of New York, described as the 'rotten apple'. In a story entitled 'Wasted Lives', the US (and the 'rampant corruption and gross inefficiency' of its reconstruction work in Iraq) is blamed when poverty-stricken Iraqis are forced to make ends meet by raking through mounds of waste. For these innocent people, 'life is literally rubbish'. The piece opens at Baghdad's landfill, and two children who begin this and every day by sorting through it for something to salvage and sell. 'The reward for carting 40 pounds of trash around? Two dollars and fifty cents', says the reporter, who then comes into view, standing in front of 'acres of Baghdad's trash'. He explains that the site may appear to be only waste, but to many it is both livelihood and home. Before the American intervention, they lived in proper houses and felt safe. 'The American occupation turned Iraq into a battlefield as well as sowing the seeds of political corruption,' insists Faizia Al-Obaidiy, identified as an MP (although her party is not given). 'How can Americans stand back and watch without intervening in this situation?' she asks, as the camera rests on the impish gaze of a scruffy but beautiful child. 'Experts' worry about the fate of children growing up on the garbage dumps, says the reporter. A masked youth is interviewed as saying that all he wants is to be able to go home. The reporter closes by saying this is impossible, as it is no longer safe: the American intervention put a wedge between the Shias whose lives are wasted and their Sunni neighbours of the past. 'Children like Fatma will continue to collect trash in order to survive.'

The fate of children who are casualties of violent conflict between neighbours is the focus of a story broadcast on AJE in May 2014. The space of this narrative is not one of waste, however, and the theme is one of hope and change rather than inevitable alienation.

The course of rehabilitation

The topic of the report is the fate of the thousands of children who were kidnapped and forced to fight for Joseph Kony's Lord's Resistance Army. It begins in Kitgum, Uganda, where a young man is packing his suitcase in an empty dormitory, preparing to go home after 13 years in captivity. The reporter, who is heard but not seen, explains that Dennis Ocan was abducted from his village when he was 10 years old, and forced to become a soldier and to commit atrocities. Dennis explains that many of the children were beaten to death, and that they had to follow orders to avoid being killed by the warlords. A simple but tidy shack, identified by the reporter as the World Vision Rehabilitation Centre, comes into view, and the camera pans walls filled with childish murals of people playing, and of automatic rifles. Viewers are told that an estimated 10 thousand abducted children are still missing, but that a trickle of former child soldiers, now adults, manage to escape. They are brought to the centre where they receive counselling from a woman, who is interviewed, but only briefly. The narrative belongs to Dennis.

The time has come for him to return to the family and neighbours he last saw when he was a boy. We watch him pack his bags, then leave with them, as the reporter's voice explains that Dennis was forced to march hundreds of kilometres, across four different countries. Dennis puts his bag in a jeep, it pulls away, and in the next shot, the viewer is placed beside him in the vehicle. As Dennis looks out at the red and green countryside fleeting across the background, the reporter explains he has seen and done things he does not want to talk about. Many child soldiers were forced to kill their relatives or neighbours, and are scared to go home. They don't know how people will react.

The moment these words are uttered, dozens of villagers can be seen running towards Dennis—and us—jubilating, with arms raised in the air and hands waving in welcome. The reporter explains the people came running two kilometres from the village, and made Dennis tread on an egg—a ritual of reconciliation. We stand beside him as he does this, and as men from the village shake his hand. For the first time, the reporter comes into view, addressing the viewer from the midst of the crowd. 'There's no grudges here,' he says. 'He's safe'.

In this narrative, a figure who could be cast as a monster is given a human face. The boy who has been outside for 13 years, who has witnessed and perhaps committed atrocities, appears as a polite and well-dressed young man, who is welcomed back to his home. The space of the story is not just rehabilitation centre and village but a moving vehicle, and the metaphor of the journey is central to the narrative. It is significant that Dennis is first encountered at a transition point or liminal space, for in contrast to the dead end of the Baghdad dump, anything is possible on this threshold. What makes this a cosmopolitan narrative is the positioning of the viewer in the moving car beside Dennis, and then at his side as reconciliation is enacted. The vantage point of the village is antithesis of the 'high-helicopter' view, and space is used to fashion a narrative that is anything but 'objective'. The viewer is firmly situated on the side of peace, freedom and reconciliation. Not all AJE narratives are like this, however.

Rodeo rehab

A week after Dennis returns to his Ugandan village, another AJE reporter takes viewers to the US state of Louisiana, where 'rodeos are a big part of rural life in the south'. The space of this narrative is the Angolan Prison Rodeo, where prisoners get a chance to win money if they can survive a stampede or stay on a bucking bronco. The story opens to the sight of a corral door swinging open and a huge raging bull charging towards a table in the middle of the ring, around which four black men in prison stripes are seated. They are immediately scattered, one is tossed in the air by the horns of the bull and another is trampled. The reporter explains that the men are inmates at one of the state's most secure prisons, some of them rapists and murderers. They are all black. 'This is part of the rehabilitation programme and part of our re-entry', says the warden of the penitentiary, a large white man. 'We gotta try to rehabilitate them so if any of them get out they don't hurt you again'.

Locals call the prison 'Angola'. The staff decline to say how many prisoners have been hurt over the years, and there is little sympathy for the convicted criminals who volunteer to take part. 'They got a choice' says a white man who has come to watch the spectacle, 'just like they had a choice what they was doing'. More than half the prisoners, says the reporter, are first-time offenders 'who will never see the outside of these prison walls': the average sentence is 95 years. 'Most of these men will die and be buried here', concludes the reporter, as a man is thrown from a bucking bronco and trampled. 'For them, this rodeo is a taste of freedom. Even if it's only for a few seconds.'

The space around which this narrative is structured is quite different from the space in the narrative of Dennis, the other prisoner undergoing rehabilitation. The space of this narrative is guarded—by protective gates at the rodeo (restraining the raging bulls) and, in intermediate shots, but the barbed wire surrounding the penitentiary. The black men in need of rehabilitation are confined within these spaces, where they are watched by prison guards and members of the public who come to watch the spectacle. The fact that the prison is called Angola is remarked upon several times, and thus reinforces the situating of the story in the 'South'. While the black inmates remain voiceless in this story, and are viewed at a distance—tossed in the air by the horns of a bull or trampled by the hooves of a wild horse—they are not the 'others', it could be argued. By contrasting this method of rehabilitation with the more humane treatment by Ugandans of Dennis, it is the white Americans who come across as strange and inhuman, rather like the inhabitants of Panem, the ruling class of the centre, who delight in the spectacle of *The Hunger Games*. The space of Angola is closed and static—not open and forward-moving, as in Uganda.

Cosmopolitan geographies

Dharwadker (2001: 10) has suggested that village and city 'are as vital to the life of cosmopolitanism as individual nations and the collective order of nations'. In a similar way, the stories of the margins—of the village or south—can provide more nourishment for a cosmopolitan outlook, more compellingly, than elite- and state-focused accounts of world politics, or narratives of the centre. The narrative techniques of Al Jazeera English journalists, who take their viewers to the space of the margins and invite them to listen to the voice of the voiceless, can be seen as an instance of the locally- inflected global journalism solicited by Berglez (2013). The world refracted by the Russia Today screen, on the other hand, is both one that is state-centric, and divided between 'the West' (the US, UK and Europe) and 'the Rest' (Russia, and critics of the US, UK and EU). The setting of RT and AJE accounts of the world are quite different. One is a global world of shared problems; the other is a cold-war world of geopolitical divides.

Space, as explicated by Adams and Jansson (2012) is used to structure stories considered here that focus on reversed flows, from colonial centre to now-booming periphery. The Lisbon of the AJE story, with its port and sea view and statues of pioneering travellers, is a place of both material and symbolic cosmopolitanism. The narrative technique that results in the viewer sharing the experiences of Dennis in Uganda—listening and journeying with him—uses place to relate layered, subjective experience grounded in the local experience of the rehabilitation centre and the traumatized, yet forgiving, village.

Less subtly, RT journalists inscribe meaning in the places they invite their viewers to visit too. Struggling to survive a poorly managed economic crisis, the place of the West is the garbage dump. Huxley's theme of alienation runs throughout RT reports of a US and Europe in crisis. *Brave New World* was 'full of barbed wit and malice-spiced frankness' (Observer), characterised by 'derisive logic' (*The Times*) and 'equally a denunciation of capitalism and communism' (*Daily Telegraph*). Apart from the fact that the novel was also a brilliant critique, the same descriptors could be applied to RT discourse. It is often fanciful, but usually contains a fact or uses a real and recognizable problem as a news handle, and obviously uses real people who are interviewed saying what they believe. RT's othering techniques reside in how newsreader and reporter structure their reports around these truths, and around stereotypes of the West in general and UK in particular as hypocritical, unjust and in trouble: there is homogeneity rather than narrative diversity in play here. In its rhetorical strategies there is also evidence of soft power games—of strategic narratives that cast Russia in a favourable light by implicitly contrasting it with its counterpart.

A distinctive feature of AJE reports is the use of maps to locate and ground its narratives, as Caquard (2011) would put it. Maps are used, not just to connect the viewer and the person with a story to tell (be it reporter or a person interviewed in the report), but also to show the disconnect between the space of the European centre (where candidates for the presidency are debating in an arena) and the ordinary space of the neighbourhood. The narratives that chronicle failing global structures and incoherence in the workings of a hegemonic market, remarked upon by Orgad 2012 and Couldry 2010, are clearly discernible in the discourse of RT. There is ridicule here, not of infantilized Greeks and Spaniards, but of the EU and the governments of the US and UK (as well as ordinary Americans and Britons).

The two AJE stories about the rehabilitation of black men who have committed violent crimes are examples of how otherness can be grasped in terms of contrasts, in the Saussurean sense (i.e. red is not-blue). Americans are 'other' in the piece about the rodeo, because the justice system can be seen to be unjust, and its rehabilitation measures as non-rehabilitation, when contrasted with the Ugandan method that Dennis, the former boy soldier, experiences. 'Proper distance' preserves the other through difference (the average viewer can never know what it means to be a child soldier who has been kidnapped and forced to commit atrocities) but also creates understanding through proximity (when the viewer is positioned by his side as he travels from the intermediate space of the rehabilitation centre home to the village, and invited to celebrate his return from the dead). Hallin is right: the use of place as setting has considerable power and is not objective. But, it could be argued, it is more adequate to a complex world than the 'balanced' but abstract reports that emanate from the press conference rather than the field. The semiotic material analysed here is remarkably different from what Hallin seems to have in mind (US newspapers, often local), but illustrates well why Hall thought that global communication can destabilize understandings of where we belong, and who we stand beside.

Reflecting on what 'cosmopolitan reading' entails, Appiah observes that smart, well-educated American students feel no embarrassment when admitting that they are unfamiliar with the plot of *The Tempest*. He regrets this, as 'we travel in books to learn mutual toleration' (Appiah 2001: 203). Stories must be shared if we are to move on and broaden our horizons. African novels, he notes, were written by people who read English, French and American literature. When reading in 'a cosmopolitan spirit', however, 'the form in which our travel comes is not the moment of the first encounter, an ethnographic ground zero, but is rather the literary equivalent of the safari' (2001: 206). Using a different metaphor than the safari, we could instead imagine returning, time and again, to a table at a café in the square of a faraway town, from which vantage point people can be observed walking or scurrying past, overheard speaking to their companions or on their mobile phones. It is these repeated encounters that news media—local, national or global—can provide a space for, which means that an analytical focus on particular stories has inevitable limitations.

Be that as it may, the cosmopolitanism that Appiah wants to defend is not a dialogue among static, closed cultures. He is not interested in a common theoretical understanding that people have a common nature, but rather in 'an invitation to respond in imagination to narratively constructed situations' involving difference. The capacity to construct a world to which our imaginations respond 'is to be found up the Amazon, the Mississippi, the Congo, the Indus, and the Yellow Rivers, just as it is found on the banks of the Avon and the Dordogne' (2001: 223). But what makes cosmopolitan conversations possible, he writes, is not shared culture or universal principles. It is 'the capacity to follow a narrative and conjure a world' (2001: 224). The world conjured in the next and penultimate chapter is a surprising one, not least because it is viewed through the eyes of others, from the vantage point of the third space.

· 5 ·

ANOTHER WORLD

Europe as Other

'If Europe is an imagined community at all,
it is never better imagined than from the outside'.[53]

Caquard (2011) explored counter-narratives of place-making by focussing on the words that subjugated people used in response to dominant Western ideologies. This chapter examines an instance of such counter-narratives, and looks into a third space—a liminal, marginal space—of the sort that has concerned scholars working in the post-colonial tradition. Its founding father, Edward Said, wrote that Europe had constructed an image of its South, over the centuries, that was more about Europe itself than the culture it exoticised Said (1978/2003). His notion of 'strategic location' describes the position of an author in a text in relation to the material about the stranger being depicted, and ordered.

> Everyone who writes about the Orient must locate himself vis-à-vis the Orient; translated into his text, this location includes the kind of narrative voice he adopts, the type of structure he builds, the kinds of images, themes, motifs that circulate in his text—all of which add up to deliberate ways of addressing the reader… (Said 1978/2003: 20).

Chapter 4 contained an illustration of the literal reversing of flows—from Germany to Turkey and from Portugal to Angola. This chapter considers the possibility of a reversed Orientalism, if 'the Orient' is taken in a broad sense to signify part of the world once under colonial dominion and treated as exotic. In focus is a series of programmes that were broadcast on AJE in 2011 and which are still available online as this book goes to print, *Surprising Europe*.[54] The narratives analysed here, then, are not drawn from regular news bulletins, but they were part of the output provided by this 24-hour news channel, and for a purpose. As one AJE news executive put it, 'There's a reason why Al Jazeera isn't just a news channel, why we don't just have a pure news channel and a documentary channel. It's because, for the viewer, they're watching everything and they're getting a whole rounded experience ...It's an attempt to address difference'.[55]

Appadurai (1996) has famously argued that imagination has become social practice and 'the key component of the new global order'. In his mediascapes, repertoires of images and narratives are offered that can be used to make sense of how our lives relate to those of others. In this order, 'codifications of both Self and Other' are being transformed (Delanty 2006: 37). Stevenson (2003) insists that a key structural division in a globalized world is the control of the powerful over dominant discourses and frameworks of understanding, and Pieterse (2009) says the 'rise of the rest' has been difficult for Western media to address because it does not fit into their national narratives. *Surprising Europe* can serve as an illustration of how 'the transformation of codifications of Self and Other' can be achieved in practice, and of narrative techniques that literally reverse the gaze. The double entendre in the name of the series refers, on the one hand, to how 'Europe' can be surprised by the advent of people who do not take its modus operandi for granted and, on the other, to how Europe can look surprisingly different when seen through the eyes of people who come to it from across the water. *Surprising Europe* is approached in this chapter as a nest of narratives: the series as a whole; the nine programmes it is comprised of; and the component stories and testimonies within each of those programmes. Picking up from where the last chapter left off, they show how othering techniques can be an important feature of cosmopolitan narratives, rather than their antithesis. They also constitute an invitation to think about whether Said's notion of 'orientalism' could be reworked and reapplied in the multivalent context of a global media flows.

As set out earlier, the literature on cosmopolitanism is increasingly seen as having a moral dimension, in its concern with the Other;

> the Other across media space, the Other represented and representing, the Other invisible in media space, the Other disabled and distorted (Ong 2009: 450).

The notion of a 'third space', first mentioned in Chapter 4, is thought by postcolonial scholars to be the most productive of all communicative spaces (Bhabha 1990). In this space of the margins, the hybrid individual (which is perhaps a more useful way of thinking about the consumers of global media messages and the people who move about and live in a globalized world than Beck's default cosmopolitans) engages in quotidian conversation with the Other. Appiah (2001) has argued that such everyday conversations, and 'repeated encounters with difference in the banality of daily life' can transform our relations with others over time. Pinchevsky, on the other hand (reading Levinas) claims that it is not in the routine encounter, but in 'breaks' and 'interruptions' in communication, that we have the most genuine encounters with the Other (cited in Ong 2009: 461). The semiotic material analysed in this chapter contains interactions of both sorts.

In earlier chapters, the notion of witnessing (Peters 1999, 2009; Frosh & Pinchevsky 2009) was put to use in the analysis of narrative techniques that can be thought to form discursive connections between the people taking part in tumultuous events and viewers watching those events unfold in real time from screens in distant homes and workplaces. This notion, it will be recalled, seeks to capture the dynamics of what happens when people bear witness in media reports, and when those reports are crafted in such a way that audiences are positioned, in turn, as witnesses (Peters 2009: 24). It is a device that can be put to work not only at times of crisis and in conflictual settings, but also in conveying a sense of the everyday challenges and perspectives of people in our midst, whom we might not otherwise see. Whether performed by a media professional or ordinary person, media witnessing represents a shared world, 'shared, that is, by both viewers and those depicted' (Frosh & Pinchevsky 2009: 10).

One of the main arguments of this book is that television continues to be a key site for such sharing. However they are distributed (by cable, website, YouTube or podcast) or consumed (on stationary or mobile device), television stories are key to the imaginative work that helps us get our bearing in the world and maintain or negotiate a sense of belonging. This can largely be attributed to its narrative properties, and the human tendency to use narrative to organize experience into understanding, and as a basis for action. Scholars of narrative have thus also been helpful to those seeking to understand representation in globalized, media-saturated settings (Bruner 1991; Czarniawska 2004; Larsen 2002; Lieblich et. al. 1998; Robertson 2012). In contrast to the quantitative approach that continues to characterise many news analyses, narrative 'deals with the particular and the specific, rather than the collective and statistical' (Kiser 1996: 250). The value of this methodology nevertheless resides in its ability to provide analytical purchase on larger cultural and societal processes. As Somers (1994: 614) put it, people are guided to act in certain ways and not others 'on the basis of the projections, expectations and memories derived from a repertoire of available social, public and cultural narratives'. The imaginative interplay between the individual and the societal is what scholars of narrative try to grasp.

Some of them pay attention to the formal properties, functions and structure of narratives. Labov has identified elements common to all tales: an abstract (or summary introduction); an orientation (as to the time, place, situation and participants); a complicating action (moving the story from a major to minor key, or providing an antithesis); an evaluation (in which the meaning of the action is commented on); a resolution (telling what finally happened); and a coda that returns the perspective to the present (Labov & Waletsky 1967). Chatman's distinction between story or *histoire* (the 'what', or the events and orientation referred to by Labov) and discourse or *discours* (the 'how', or the way the story is communicated) is also helpful. While the structural approach facilitates the systematisation of different narratives into material that can be used as a basis for comparative analysis, the admonition to attend to *discours* as well as *histoire* encourages the coder to take into account the deployment of the imagery, metaphors and juxtapositions which give stories their power. It is devices such as these, together with the use of space and representation of others that featured in Chapter 4, which make it possible to internalise narratives, to carry them with us as we go about our daily tasks, and to continue to think about them once we have switched off the screen. They help us to remember as well as to know.

It has been argued elsewhere (Robertson 2010) that the power of television news narratives to do this, and to engage as well as inform, can be performed in different ways, or on different dimensions. On the first dimension, where Beck's 'latent cosmopolitanism' can be thought to originate, imaginative work makes us aware. On the second dimension, there is an appeal to the sympathy, or even pity, of the viewer, as theorised by Boltanski (1999) and Chouliaraki (2006, 2008). Beyond that, however, is a third imaginative dimension, which nourishes engagement in a deterritorialized Meyrowitzian world. When narratives invite identification, we are brought to the Other, or the Other is brought to us, and we are encouraged to imagine what it would be like to be in their stead. It is here that what Beck (2006) identifies as a constitutive principle of cosmopolitanism comes into play: the 'perspective-taking' that entails the capacity and willingness to put oneself in the position of the other.

One way of getting at othering mechanisms or perspective-taking is to look for the occurrence of different conventions in current affairs narratives on television. Graddol (1994) has identified two traditions that are used in television journalism to tell stories about the world. 'Realism' is that which is most familiar, particularly in Anglo-American outlets. According to its conventions, the reporter dominates the field of vision, and stands between viewers and the objects of the report, whose accounts are encompassed by the ominscient narrator's voice. The tradition of 'naturalism', by way of contrast, provides 'a representation of the world as it might be directly experienced by the viewer [...] From a naturalist perspective, a news report provides a vicarious experience, an image of the world as we might expect to experience it if we were to stand where the reporter stands' (Graddol 1994: 140–5). Naturalist techniques were in play in the narratives of Uganda and Angola in Chapter 4, with the reporter on site but off-screen. This is one of the reasons that such journalism is different, and arguably more powerful, than the 'objective' variety problematised earlier by Hallin (2006). The difference between realist and naturalist representation bears an affinity to the difference between the 'panoptic controlling male gaze' through which difference and distance are confirmed, and the 'mobile' gaze that Nava (2007: 25–6) characterizes as female, it has been argued, and as more conducive to a cosmopolitan outlook.

That AJE strives for this cosmopolitan gaze—a gaze that is at once mobile, in the sense that Nava uses it, but also rooted to the local context of reports—comes across in interviews conducted with journalists working for the organization.

> Our audience might be a university professor from Stockholm or an IT engineer from Jakarta or a bus driver in Buenos Aires...The common denominator is an understanding of the human experience, and the impact on people brings home the story. If you talk to any TV journalist, they'll talk about the importance of the human, but that is really something that we push here. There's quite a lot of times where people are telling their own stories, rather than the reporter telling the story. There's less reporter involvement, less of the kind of classic, usually more American way of telling the story, where the reporter is central.[56]

In analysing *Surprising Europe*, a number of simple questions have been drawn from these somewhat abstract notions. They have been posed to the narratives encoded in, and constituting, the series. The methodology of this study basically involves the attempt to answer these innocent questions, and to explain what has prompted those answers. Questions related to the imaginative dimension (awareness) are: what is happening, and who is it happening to? Trying to establish whether work on the second or third of these dimensions is in evidence, additional questions ask where the viewer is situated in these narratives. Do we find ourselves in a cellar looking up at the world or on a rooftop looking down; in a public space or a private home (orientation/place as setting)? Through whose eyes do we look at a given situation, and how does the story proceed (complicating action)? What do the answers and the interplay of *histoire* and *discours* tell us about Europe (evaluation) and what happens when the discursive gaze is reversed (coda)? All these seek answers to the more general question first posed in Chapter 4: how is Europe narrated, and perhaps othered, on *Surprising Europe*?

Seeing Europe through other eyes (orientation)

There are narratives on many levels in *Surprising Europe*. The series itself can be understood as a narrative whole, in the same way that a novel by Dickens might have been published in weekly portions, or the televised version of the novel envisaged and broadcast in weekly episodes, but is nevertheless considered to be one story. The titles of the nine programmes suggest that they together contribute to an overarching narrative: the series begins with *Taking the Leap*, about people leaving Africa in search of a better life in Europe, and ends with *Home Sweet Home*, when migrants and second-generation immigrants talk about returning. Each programme can nevertheless be seen as a narrative in itself. The programmes, in turn, consist of reports revolving around the personal narratives of African migrants in Europe. The stories are narrated in different registers, with each programme including a musical narrative, usually rap, with lyrics specifically addressing multi-cultural encounters in a European setting.

All nine programmes in the series have been analysed in their 25-minute entirety (216 minutes, all told). Each has a different African cultural worker as guest reporter, and three to five component items or stories, one of which is always a quizzical report filed by Ugandan journalist Ssuuna

Golooba. The narrative technique of naturalism is deployed throughout. The migrants whose stories form the basis of the various reports tell their experiences in their own words, without the noticeable intervention of a reporter. In some cases the address is direct: a raconteur will look straight into the camera and speak 'to all Africans who come to Europe' or a singer, in keeping with the generic conventions of the music video, will lean toward us and pull us into the setting, be it Parisian square, Roman hilltop or Berlin playground.

The host of the series is Kenyan 'artist and entrepreneur' K-Nel, who addresses viewers in a particular way. While he speaks specifically to 'African brothers and sisters', the non-African viewer does not feel like a voyeur, or someone eavesdropping on diasporic media: it is clear that this programme is aimed at the general global audience.[57] The deliberate mode of address signals a sophisticated form of othering (of which more below), and is in keeping with the AJE policy of challenging established perspectives. K-Nel is consistently cheery and upbeat throughout, even when shaking his head over the tragic stories that some of the migrants tell. At the end of most items and each programme, he invites viewers to contribute their own stories via the website, and preferably by webcam. We are given to understand that—like many contemporary media artefacts circulating in a converging environment—the narrative work is a collective and ongoing endeavour.

The first programme, *Taking the Leap*, opens with K-Nel greeting viewers from a city rooftop. In what in narrative analytical terms would be called the abstract, he introduces himself as a Kenyan who has been living in Europe for more than a decade, and says that in his experience, 'many brothers and sisters back home in Africa have no idea how we are living over here in Europe'. The intention of the series is thus to show them the good and bad sides of life in Europe 'from an African point of view'. Reporters across Europe will 'look at strange rituals' and show 'us' how love, hate and hostility can be found there. From the outset, then, an ambiguous form of audience address is established.

There are traces in the first episode suggesting that non-Africans are at least one segment of the intended audience. For example, the introduction contains an explanation of why people migrate to Europe, which is presumably superfluous information for a migrant. In this programme, viewers are taken to Africa, where they encounter Africans imagining Europe. In a church, people wave their passports in the air and pray together, as the minister promises that they will never be refused a visa. K-Nel says in a voiceover to African village scenes that 'many of us' expect Europe to bring money, freedom, and happiness. A young man on a motorbike says that

> according to the news on television we are seeing, Europe is so beautiful

and other voices, and the lyrics of a song performed by a man playing a traditional instrument in a humble room with barred windows, express visions of a Europe of dreams—of the imagination.

Plate 5.1. The Europe of the imagination. A musician in African sings about people dreaming of adventures in Europe, in the first episode of the *Surprising Europe* series, *Taking the Leap*, http://www.aljazeera.com/programmes/surprisingeurope/2011/08/20118695843266691.html. Image reproduced with permission from Witfilm, http://witfilm.nl.

The scene shifts to Malta. To shots of vast expanses of water and people adrift in small, overcrowded vessels, we are told that refugees arrive here daily. Dayo, who survived the voyage from Nigeria, explains that the empty boats he is standing beside have been left to bear witness to the ordeal. 'If they were not here, how would you believe that we came with these boats?', he asks.

'Imagine you enter the European mainland by plane or by boat', says K-Nel, when we are returned to him. Once there, no visas are needed to cross the border—except to the UK. The next story shows how migrants try to enter the country by hiding in lorries, an entrance blocked by collaborating

British and French authorities. We watch while border guards find stowaways from Afghanistan and Eritrea, and in the outro, K-Nel looks us in the eye and asks: 'Can you imagine hiding inside a cargo for days?' In the third item, rapper Scor.Pi.O., from Cameroon, sings a song in English entitled 'Surprising Europe' and speaks in Dutch about how he and his mother lived illegally for a decade—what he calls wasted years. 'It was just two of us against the government', he says.

In the next report, Ssuuna arrives in an Amsterdam lit up by fireworks on New Year's Eve. At first, he finds everyone friendly and welcoming (and perhaps a bit tipsy), but he soon encounters another side to the city. We follow him from one seedy room to another, in the company of white landlords whose faces are pixellated out, and who are charging exorbitant rents for substandard housing. In the end, he finds a tiny basement room to rent in the city centre, and makes a bed in the kitchen.

The second episode revolves around African migrants' stories of success and failure, once they have made it to Europe. K-Nel greets us as he rides up an escalator to the street level of a busy business district. In the abstract to this episode, the viewer is told that, apart from the 4.5 million Africans who officially work and study in Europe, there are 7–8 million who try to make a living without papers. From behind the desk in his travel agency, Steven talks about the importance of education, and how his first employers discouraged him from studying. Steven's locales are the luxury shops we visit while he buys perfume and jewelry, and the expensive restaurant at which we share a table, but he explains: 'When you come here it's like you've come to hell.' Michael, who has been coming to Spain as a seasonal worker for 17 years, and who is the focus of the second item, is still living in that hell. He sleeps rough, doesn't get enough to eat, and occasionally resorts to begging. We follow him through construction sites (where there is no work), into the countryside (suffering from a bad harvest) and into a camp where other Africans have gathered, to sleep and to cook around a communal fire. We are invited to bear witness: 'Look at how people are sleeping outside in these conditions', says Michael in a subdued voice, explaining that this is the Europe people in Africa don't imagine. He tells us he is a family man, with five children and a mother and sisters to support in Ghana, and he is ashamed that he has not been able to send them any money for over a year.

Plate 5.2. The Europe of directly lived experience. Michael, from Ghana, talks about the hardships of surviving in Spain in the second episode of the *Surprising Europe* series, *Hopes and Dreams*, http://www.aljazeera.com/programmes/surprisingeurope/2011/08/201186102630499582.html. Image reproduced with permission from Witfilm, http://witfilm.nl.

We also follow Ssuuna on a job hunt. He wipes babies' bottoms, cleans cars and does worse for little pay. It is difficult finding a job without the proper papers, but some businesses are willing to take the risk of employing someone like Ssuuna, we are told, as we see him lift the lid of a filthy, unflushed toilet, and flinch. Later in the programme, we learn that Lisbon is not just the home of many migrants from Angola and Mozambique, but also to kuduro, a new music style that is African and universal, as music movements are, 'when they touch people'. Excerpts from a song by one of the storytellers frames this piece, which ends with the lyrics

> This is Portugal, this is Angola. This is Lisbon, this is Luanda.

In the third episode, we meet Mopi and Emmanuel, who says

> How you imagine in Africa, that's not what it's like here.

Educated as draughtsmen in Ghana, they have ended up sleeping in a disused factory and parking cars in Valencia for €2–6 a day. K-Nel comments in the outro/evaluation that going hungry and sleeping in the rough is hard, "but the hardest part is what happens inside the heart, in the head". He hands us over to Sylvia, from Uganda. Despite having been living in Biljmer for 15 years, she is still forced to move around like a nomad. "We grow up knowing every person is a sister or a brother", she says. "But when we come to Europe, they don't like to help." Her landlady advised her to sell her body to pay the rent, but Sylvia would rather die. She has had thoughts of suicide and we follow her to the riverside where she almost took her life, and sit beside her as she weeps. She talks about the African's fear of deportation of arriving back home with absolutely nothing, to be scorned and shamed. So she stays on, and stays alive. "Why end my life because of just papers?"

Ssuuna visits a dog hotel, and is surprised to learn that Europeans pay €15 a day to board their canine family members—more than Mopi and Emmanuel make in a week—and that European dogs have passports. In this tongue-in-cheek report, the gaze is overtly reversed, and Europeans become objectified. The question of relative worth is reinforced in by Papy, who talks and sings about the difference between animals and humans. Atop a hill overlooking Rome, he contrasts his native Senegal, where no one goes hungry because everyone shares, with Europe, where people say: 'not now, we're eating'.

Plate 5.3. Living like animals. Ssuuna, from Uganda, visits a dog hotel in the Netherlands and discovers how well they live, in contrast to undocumented migrants in Europe, in the third episode of the *Surprising Europe* series, *Making Ends Meet*, http://www.aljazeera.com/programmes/surprisingeurope/2011/08/20118168557626755.html. Image reproduced with permission from Witfilm, http://witfilm.nl.

The fourth episode begins in Burkina Faso, where stereotypical huts stand beside bungalows made of bricks and plaster, which an elder explains are the homes of villagers working in Italy. The local doctor says that the new hospital, ambulances and tv sets in the village are all thanks to 'Europe', and the schoolteacher explains that Italy is

> a castle from which money flows like water.

Back in Europe, K-Nel tells us he knows many brothers and sisters do illegal things to survive. We follow a drug pusher as he plies his trade in Barcelona, and tells us, in hushed tones in his bedroom, about the religious mother who gets the money he makes, but who he can't inform of its provenance. In

Geneva, Rose recounts that she was expecting to find a job as a cleaner when she left Nigeria.

> That was what I was thinking I would find. But that is not what I found. I found prostitution in Europe.

The woman who got her into prostitution is a 'friend' from home—a common form of trafficking, we learn from the experts K-Nel enlists to 'deepen our understanding' of this complicated business.

In the episode's final piece, Ghanian Baba visits Bunyol in Spain to experience La Tomatina. He is like Ssuuna: a curious reporter investigating peculiar European practices. We walk with Baba to the town square, stand behind him as the truck with tomatoes arrives, and follow him into the thick of the tomato-throwing. 'Why are you doing this?' he asks a middle-aged Spaniard with tomato slime running down his face, and is told that it's a great way to get rid of stress. A blond woman explains that tomatoes are excellent for the skin and hair. We see girls in bikinis bathing in the vegetable carnage and a young woman lying on the street splashing tomato juice all over her nether parts. It is a playful item, but the account of 250 thousand kilos of food being wasted in a few hours contrasts jarringly with earlier tales of destitution. As Baba sums it up in the evaluation: 'It was a lot of fun but very strange for me to see people fighting with tomatoes like this at the same time people are dying of hunger.'

Plate 5.4. Europe as a strange place. Baba, from Ghana, reports from the Spanish town of Bunol, where 250 thousand kilograms of tomatoes are destroyed in a few hours of revelry, in the fourth episode of the *Surprising Europe* series, *Under Pressure*, http://www.aljazeera.com/programmes/surprisingeurope/2011/08/201183065919297868.html. Image reproduced with permission from Witfilm, http://witfilm.nl.

In the fifth episode, K-Nel observes, to the grand strains of baroque music and a shot of a royal park, that Europeans are very proud of their culture. With the arrival of so many migrants, they are worried they will lose their identity, and forget that migrants have been here for centuries ('multi-culturalism is a fact of life'). We join Mousse, a drummer from Senegal, who makes dinner for his family and changes a nappy. Being a European parent means planning every hour of the day in detail (Mousse points to the full calendar on the kitchen wall), but he has learned how to retain his African penchant for making time for people. Then the intrepid Ssuuna bundles up to observe yet another curious European custom, this time from the vantage point of a the wintry beach, where hundreds of Dutchmen have gathered in bathing suits and red toques to take a New Year's plunge. Ssuuna wears his by-now familiar bemused look and asks the pink-tinged bathers: 'Why are you doing this thing?' One young man replies: 'Life is very easy—you have to make it a little bit harder for yourself'. Spotting a group of blacks, Ssuuna concludes that they must have been in Europe too long. In the resolution, he is left warm and dry on the beach as the Dutch run into the freezing sea, and concludes: 'Today I discovered I'm not really a European yet.'

Plate 5.5. Europe as difficult to understand. Ssuuna, from Uganda, watches as Dutch bathers plunge into an icy sea on New Year's Day, in the fifth episode of the *Surprising Europe* series, *Culture Shock*, http://www.aljazeera.com/programmes/surprisingeurope/. Image reproduced with permission from Witfilm, http://witfilm.nl.

The guest reporter in the sixth episode is the Senegalese hip-hop artist Sister Fa, who rises out of the U-Bahn to greet us. 'This is a little bit like my story with my friends around me, says the woman who made her home in Berlin, with her German husband, 'and this is Europe'. We follow Sister Fa and her baby from the flat into the park, accompanied by the less fortunate Bea, whose father has confiscated her papers. Bea has to raise her child on her own, 'but that's how you do it in Europe'. We visit Samuel, whose student visa has expired and which can't be renewed, despite his having lived with a German girl for two years. He packs his bags, descends the stairs and says:

> The Europe I knew was the Europe I saw on television. I thought Germany was the dominant power in Europe in which I would have the chance to succeed.

K-Nel then announces he will 'take you to a place you don't want to go': the detention centre in Zeist. Although it is obviously a prison—with high walls and barbed wire and security cameras, we are told these people are not criminals. The theme of humans being treated like animals returns and is indeed explicitly referred to as detainees tell their stories.

Plate 5.6. Unbelievable Europe. An innocent migrant is kept at the detention centre in Zeist in the sixth episode of the *Surprising Europe* series, *Running Out of Luck*, http://www.aljazeera.com/programmes/surprisingeurope/. Image reproduced with permission from Witfilm, http://witfilm.nl.

Back in London, K-Nel reminds us that he promised us a happy ending to this episode, 'which has been full of sorrow and hardships'. It is provided, as ever, by Ssuuna, who 'is on a research tour, looking for ways that Europeans cope with their problems'. One of these is stress. To Keystone-Cops music and cityscapes played on fast-forward, Ssuuna explains that the Netherlands is a rich country, and the people work very hard.

> They have good houses, hospitals, and all children go to school. I would expect the people to be happy but they don't look happy. How come? These people are working so hard, they forgot how to be happy. But these people are very creative. They have a solution to any problem.

We are suddenly surprised to see and hear white people lying on the grass, laughing hysterically. Ssuuna stands looking down at them, baffled, then glances up at us as if to see if we know what to make of it. 'First I thought they were on drugs', he says. 'Then I found out they were doing something called laugh therapy.' He asks a man whether it is true, that in Europe one must take lessons to learn how to laugh, and answered in the affirmative. In the coda, Ssuuna observes that he was born a happy man, and wonders whether he should ask for some money for his laughter. In a new twist on the rich-man/poor-man theme, he wanders off through the park asking himself whether he should charge ten or twenty euros an hour for his natural talent for happiness.

In the seventh episode, we hear the story of Ssissoko from Mali, who survived the conflagration that claimed 20 lives in a firetrap in Pompiers de Paris, and who subsequently founded an association to warn and protect Africans living in similar conditions. Gabonese rapper Lord Ekomy sings to us in and around the Eiffel Tower, and takes us to meet undocumented migrants who united to have their voices heard, gathering in the disused government building known as 'the Ministry of the Undocumented'. And we go to Brescia, an Italian town that had always welcomed migrants, until populist parties gained a foothold. Omi tells us how industrious the African neighbourhood community of Prealpino was until its members were suddenly evicted in the night, and had to watch while their building was demolished.

In the eighth episode, we get to meet K-Nel in a different role, as he assumes the narrator's stance and tells his own story. He looks at us differently now, and is the serious rapper rather than the cheery host. He talks and works on his song, one of the lines of which confirms the impression that there is a double entendre in the title of the series:

> I came to Germany as a surprise for Europe…

The battle you face as a migrant, says, K-Nel is not material: it's psychological. It is a theme that resonates with the story of Marjorie, who escaped war in Africa, where her eldest child still lives. She speaks quietly of her torture in a Ugandan prison, but mostly about being interrogated in the UK as part of her application for asylum. She sits in a window high up in a building; behind her a typical London street can be glimpsed down below. Her application for asylum was turned down. She appealed and found herself compelled to give detailed accounts of her torture and rape. The judge believed her this time, but the Home Office appealed his ruling. 'I always say that the government here, or the system, tortures people diplomatically' is Marjorie's evaluation. After being granted citizenship, she recalls: 'I looked at that piece of paper and thought: "for the last seven years, this is what I've been waiting for". For the last seven years I've not seen my child'.

The first African to become a mayor in Eastern Europe is the next storyteller. A doctor in a seaside Slovenian town, Peter is convinced that when the townspeople see him, they see a person, not an immigrant or a black man. 'Somehow, over the years, I crossed the colour barrier.' In this story, Peter is the one with status, a stately office and a medical practice. The whites he stops to speak with have less glamorous occupations, be they hairdresser or fisherman. Peter says European politicians have much to learn from Africans. 'There is a big debate in Europe about multiculturalism—what is it? As soon as one leader says it doesn't work, another follows, and so on. That's fashion politics, that's not real politics. Real politics is what you do for people.'

'Today I have come to what Europeans call an "old people's home"' announces Ssuuna, back in Holland. He accompanies an elderly couple to their flat, the camera angle inviting the viewer to think of the tower blocks and perhaps even detention centres of previous episodes, although the building is clean and bright and its inhabitants affluent. Ssuuna expresses surprise that the couple don't live with any of their four children or eight grandchildren.

Plate 5.7. Lonely Europe. Ssuuna visits an old folk's home in the Netherlands, where the elderly live instead of with their children and grandchildren, in the eighth episode of the *Surprising Europe* series, *The Good Life*, http://www.aljazeera.com/programmes/surprising-europe/. Image reproduced with permission from Witfilm, http://witfilm.nl.

In the final episode, we meet a woman who has been in Europe for 16 years. Resplendent in pure white African clothing and turban, Binata tells how she trained as a bookkeeper in France, and went to Spain in search of work. She didn't find it and ended up an undocumented street vendor who braids tourists' hair on the beach. Without papers, she is always hiding, always running. Desperately homesick but too ashamed to return to Senegal, she says she would rather have respect than money. Annie is also clad in white, but stands in sharp contrast to Binata. She 'is not ashamed at all about her desire to go back to Africa, maybe because she has never been there'. Born in Italy to Liberian parents, she has found happiness and a new musical style in her union with Francesco, who goes with her to her parents' house, kisses her father and sits down to eat with the family. 'Francesco respects me', Annie explains. 'As an African, and Francesco as an Italian, we want to give the message to people that we can all get together.' The item ends with a line from her song, performed in front of Rome's most famous cultural landmark:

Plate 5.8. Africa Surprising Europe. Italian-born Annie, who longs to 'return' to Liberia, stands in the centre of Rome and sings 'This is Africa, surprising Europe' in the ninth and final episode of the *Surprising Europe* series, *Home Sweet Home*, http://www.aljazeera.com/programmes/surprisingeurope/2011/10/20111049374961442.html. Image reproduced with permission from Witfilm, http://witfilm.nl.

In the penultimate story, Evariste leaves Europe for Burkina Faso after years of homesickness. We join him at the party he gives in his village for friends and family upon his return, when he is rather plump. He sets up a rudimentary gym and obviously uses it, because when we revisit him some time later, he has lost his fat and acquired bulging muscles. At home he has become strong. Men visit his gym and talk about their dreams and plans of migrating, and in one scene, the men of the village sit in a circle and talk about Europe. Evariste tells them this place exists only in their imaginations.

> It is a dream: The West, Europe... You watch it on the television and you think: This is it. But the reality is different.

K-Nel takes his leave at the train station. The programme—and the series—ends with talking heads from the website. The last word is from a woman who says she imagined

> a beautiful place with tall buildings and houses. It is totally different. But it is a beautiful place.

It was a lot of fun but very strange (discussion/evaluation/resolution)

The orientation of the overarching narrative is a Europe comprised of detention centres, cramped hovels and basement flats, border crossings, nightclubs, and the rooms where rap artists write their texts. Europe is parking lots, disused factories, tower blocks, football fields, living and dining rooms, streets and cafés. It is an African village in which the Italian flag flies on the hospital and African huts stand side by side with the brick homes of sons working in Europe; the shops of Barcelona; the red-light district of Geneva; and a picturesque town square filled with happy Spaniards covering each other in tomato juice. In several episodes, Europe is a place of contrasts: a place of travel agencies, luxury shops and expensive restaurants, but also of camps for the homeless, basements and public toilets. The successful businessman and the student move through their milieux in cars and trains, while the Africans who lack papers walk the streets. Classrooms and recording studios occupy an intermediate space.

Architectural metaphors structure the narratives throughout. Bureaucratic Europe is symbolized by the long corridor and closed door of the detention centre in Zeist. The quintessentially French Eiffel Tower is juxtaposed with the dwellings of Africans, neglected by absent landlords, that burn down or are torn down. Where Africans once lived in Paris and Brescia, there is now a high fence keeping them away from the new, better buildings under construction. This architectural imagery unfolds parallel to a recurrent theme in the testimonies shared in the episode: that tougher regulations are making it harder for migrants, as employers are now subject to prosecution if caught using literally black labour.

The migrants speak to us from close quarters, in their bedrooms, living rooms, kitchens and music rooms. From this perspective, we see Europe from the inside-out. K-Nel, on the other hand, speaks to us from city rooftops and squares and streets. His sites are all above-ground public places, from which he cheerfully introduces 'brothers and sisters' who inhabit basements, hovels, and tents, and invites other migrants to share their stories.

One scene makes a noticeable exception. Segueing between stories of desperation experienced by Africans without papers, K-Nel speaks to us from a courtyard surrounded by closed doors. A high gate is behind him, open slightly, leading to a brighter place. It is a concise metaphor for this narrative of Europe.

These are among the repertoire of images that are repeatedly drawn on throughout the series. Another is stairs and escalators with Africans going up and down. Water, and the bridges and boats that go with it, are recurrent images in television news reporting of migration and refugees in general, and used in a specific way in *Surprising Europe*. The imagery can suggest connections (bridges bring people and places together) or have more desolate associations. People who move, for one reason or another, from their native climes can often find themselves 'at sea', especially if they are migrants or asylum-seekers encountering bureaucracies and in need of the right papers. Bodies of water also signal a disconnect. Faced with such an image, the viewer can reasonably find herself feeling reluctant about encountering the Other. It is easy to imagine getting cold and wet, or even going under, when attempting to cross the water to engage with whoever or whatever is on the other side.

Apart from these images, the overarching *discours* of the series, in this reading, is structured around two sets of recurrent juxtapositions. One is loneliness (loneliness in Europe and the loneliness of Europeans) versus community (and more particularly the community of 'brothers and sisters' who take care of each other). The other is the divide between those who have papers, and those who lack them. The stories all centre on those without, and the people with papers are the Others, narratively marginalized and rendered invisible.

Europe is progress, Africa is respect (coda)

What insights do these narratives, and this reading of them, give into the question of difference in global media discourse? The most important is related to the finding that a particular discourse is established by the end of the series. The viewer learns to think and refer to certain problems in ways that were perhaps strange before tuning into *Surprising Europe*. Specific countries and cities are mentioned, but the primary and recurrent identities are supranational: the key concepts are 'Europe' and 'Africa', and the key players are 'Europeans' and 'African migrants'. The people who bear witness, and whose stories we share, are Africans, but they are European Africans—in contrast to the families they have left behind. The viewer also learns to think of the Africans in Europe not as illegal, but as undocumented. The most important juxtaposition in the series is not the 'us' and the 'them' that is the focus of much scholarship on othering practices, or even the divide between rich and poor. It is between those who have papers and those who do not.

Something worth reflecting on is that, while *Surprising Europe* is a very political series, politicians and parties and political processes are conspicuous by their absence. What we see is people. The political is depicted as being about relationships rather than structures. As a white hairdresser in the Slovenian seaside town says of the black mayor: he, unlike previous white incumbents, 'has a real relationship with people.'

This analysis has established that five types of Others populate the Europe depicted in this series.

Malevolent Others are invisible and know what they are doing. They are the government (that has wasted a decade of Scor.Pi.O's young life), the Home Office (which rapes people like Marjorie diplomatically), and the Ministry of the Undocumented (a metaphor, as well as a site, for the faceless bureaucracies that threaten migrants in Europe). Unscrupulous landlords and employers who exploit the undocumented also conform to this type, be they the landlady who suggested Sylvia go on the game to earn rent money, the owner of the Parisian firetrap that Ssissoko almost lost his life in, or the various dubious types that Ssuuna encounters when looking for accommodation and work. German racists are among the Malevolent Others, as are 'friends' from home who trick African women like Rose into prostitution.

Excluding Others are also invisible, but they don't necessarily act on purpose—or at all. These are the Europeans who don't need papers, and don't realize how essential they are. They are the people who Papy compares to animals, and who don't like to be disturbed by people's suffering while eating. They are the people who don't see that Binata is a trained accountant, as they pay her to braid their hair on the beach, and they are the children and grandchildren who don't have room for the elderly Dutch couple.

Familiar Others are glimpsed in the background. They are the family members who have stayed at home, stretch their hands out for money, and fail to understand the sacrifices made by the sons and daughters they have sent to Europe, or the shame they induce. They are Michael's children and sisters; they are the god-fearing mothers of the drug peddler and the prostitute; they are Evariste's wife.

Europeans are Strange Others, visible and objectified. They are people who pay for their dogs to have passports and stay in hotels; people who delight in wasteful orgies of tomato-throwing; people who plunge into frigid seas on New Year's Day because life lacks challenges; and people who have to take courses to learn how to laugh.

Finally, there is the Other Audience. K-Nel purports to be speaking to fellow Africans, and undoubtedly is, but he is also speaking to the many non-African viewers of Al Jazeera English throughout the world. By refraining from acknowledging this, non-Africans are implicitly othered. Our cicerone through this different European tour is friendly and welcoming, so the impression given is of playful irony rather than exclusion, but the non-African viewer is nevertheless situated in the position of auditor, rather than interlocutor.

The narrative techniques employed in this series result, I would argue, in sophisticated representations and challenging perspective-taking that give insights into new work of the global imagination. They give cause to rethink 'othering' as something inevitably negative and unidirectional, flowing from the West to the Rest, and illustrate how it can in practice be multi-directional and polysemic.

· 6 ·

A WORLD OF DIFFERENCE

Atlas Shrugged, which opened Chapter 3, was the product of the upheavals of the early 20th century. The stories explored in this book are the product of newsrooms located on different pages of the atlas, and upheavals of the early 21st century. They emanate from a communicative space that straddles the boundary between conflict and cosmopolitanism and speak of a different place as well as a different time.

Two decades before Rand's novel was published, the English playwright and social commenter J.B. Priestley made a documentary entitled *We Live in Two Worlds*. In writing of cosmopolitanism and the media, Tomlinson found himself revisiting the film and thinking about the contrast between 'the old world order of international divisions and political hostilities' and 'what Priestley regarded as an emerging world of internationalism and cosmopolitan progress' (Tomlinson 2011: 349–50). In Tomlinson's reading, 'the film constructs the positive idea of internationalism via a contrast with the "negative other"—the "narrow national world of angry borders"' (Tomlinson 2011: 351). A decade-and-a-half into the new millennium, it is clear that Priestley's emerging world has not replaced the old order, and that we continue to live in two worlds, both the real world in which desperate migrants drown when trying to reach the shores of Europe in overcrowded boats and the Swedish navy hunts Russian submarines on the Stockholm waterfront, and the imaginative worlds constituted by media reports of politics and society.

Silverstone's mediapolis is a useful way of conceiving one of those worlds—the global mediaspace of the imagination—and the discursive power of the people who fill it with stories. Like Lucy, who finds that the wardrobe has no end and stumbles into Narnia without realizing it, or the little girl in Spielberg's *Poltergeist* who disappears into another dimension while sitting in front of the television, I would like to suggest that we enter, through the many screens we use, a shared space in which we experience together events as they unfold—a place where the familiar relation between time and space is not necessarily abolished, but may become disjointed. In this space, we develop 'a sense of there being an elsewhere; a sense of that elsewhere being in some way relevant to me; a sense of my being there', in the words of Silverstone (2007: 10). To inhabitants of this space, whatever our actual geographical coordinates may be, what happens in Egypt, Syria, Nigeria or Brazil is our business (as it was put by one AJE journalist). This is not an intrinsic feature of global news, however—no more than it is of the local and national news media that Berglez writes of. Whether or not we are invited to feel that we are 'there' depends on what broadcasts we follow.

It could be said that the worlds depicted in the four global channels studied here bear the traits of parallel universes, not unlike the two Cambridges in *His Dark Materials* by Philip Pullman—another of the novelists whose work is replete with political overtones. The RT world, for example, seems like part of Priestley's older order of international divisions and political hostilities. By focusing on people rather than states and political elites, the AJE world appears more cosmopolitan. These and other differences, it has been argued, make it inappropriate to refer to 'global news' as if it were a reasonably coherent entity or, in some accounts, commodity. One argument that runs throughout the book is the need for empirical engagement with what is actually going on in global newsrooms, and what the people who work there think about it.

To sum up, here is the main news in brief

Both the interviews with journalists and the analysis of news broadcasts showed that some comparisons are more meaningful than others. There is considerable respect at AJE for the BBC, and a great deal in common between the two organizations. Of all the global newsrooms, these two are the best resourced, have the greatest reach, deploy armies of correspondents in the field, and have reputations for competent, reliable journalism. There are also interesting differences, that matter to the issues addressed in these pages, and one conclusion is that it is the output of these two organizations that can be most fruitfully compared in future studies. When it comes to the 'counter-hegemonics' (neither of which uses the term except to designate the other), RT compares itself with CNN, and the people in the AJE newsroom distance themselves firmly from their Russian counterpart. Several aspects of the scholarly critique rehearsed in Chapter 2 resonate in both newsrooms, however, not least the view that mainstream global media based in the Anglo-Saxon world 'question less' rather than more (to paraphrase RT's motto), by dutifully reporting the government line in their coverage of international affairs, using government members and policy elites as key sources and, often, as primary definers, and, particularly in the case of CNNI, filling their broadcasts with 'talking heads' rather than investigating the impact of the policies that the heads are talking about on non-elites in countrysides, villages and city neighbourhoods throughout the world. The advertisements that punctuate its broadcasts repeatedly enjoin the audience to 'go beyond borders with CNN', but the regular viewer nevertheless spends more time in the newsroom, with Hala Gorani and the people she chats with, than out in the field, and is being continually taken back to Washington for a reaction. The BBCW viewer gets the same treatment, and that newsroom's classically competent, reliable news reports are so often filed by a white man in his prime, with a UK accent, that in coding work for this study, the additional category of 'MAE' was added for when coding reporters. (It stands for middle-aged Englishman.) The results of such coding corroborate the study by Dencik (2013) and resonate with what AJE correspondents who had worked at the BBC had to say. As one put it:

> I'm not the only woman at the BBC saying it was a frustrating place to work. I'm not the only person saying the BBC had what felt like on the inside a masculine vibe, an element of old boys network to it […] You did feel at the BBC very strongly that it always had been a masculine environment with things tweaked to suit the make way of working, and you had to be exceptionally good as a woman to get a fair share of it, whereas you only had to be average as a bloke.[58]

When it comes to AJE, the existence of what Cottle and Rai (2008a) defined as communicative frames—overarching ways of seeing and telling that prevail in a given newsroom culture—are clearly discernible, both in how its journalists talk about what they do, and in the reports they produce. Particularly striking is the contrasting of the 'high helicopter' view to that of the village; the voiceless being given a voice; and in reversing of the gaze, if not the flow. These results, taken together with the different frames traced to the other newsrooms, shed light on what Cottle and Rai refer to as the 'communicative architecture' of television journalism, and on how it might structure the 'wider play' of power and culture (2008a: 94).

The book's focus has made it possible to consider whether the global newsroom has an architecture that is distinct from the national ones that Cottle and Rai had in mind. It transpires that they are not. The study reported here confirms what Dencik found—that BBC news produced for a domestic British audience has the same distinctive features as BBC news that is produced for a global audience—and establishes that the communicative architectures of the RT and AJE newsrooms reflect quite different relations to political power. When speaking to new executives from RT, and watching and analyzing RT broadcasts, it is obvious that the frame of reference is the Anglo-Saxon world and, specifically, the US and UK. By way of contrast, AJE news executives and journalists, when speaking of their work, consistently draw on examples and illustrations from all over the world. One clear finding of this study is thus that there are more differences than similarities between these two news organizations, despite them often being consigned to the same category of 'counter-hegemonic media'. It could indeed be said that there is a world of difference between them.

RT news broadcasts are structured by a Cold War frame, and RT discourse is a textbook example of the 'strategic narratives' that can be seen as part of states' soft power arsenals. As will be recalled from the book's introduction, strategic narratives describe how the world is structured and who makes it work, and reflect the values of the state in international relations (Roselle et al. 2014). In the world of RT, most things that go wrong are the fault of the US, UK and EU, and the market forces that underpin them (which is not necessarily a problem, in this newsworld, because everything is going terribly badly for these countries, capitalism is in decline, and the days of Western hegemony are numbered). In some periods, it is the US that most often bears the brunt of RT censure, but more often it is the UK. As well as the perpetrators of social injustices, these countries are also laughing stock, providing material for what RT executive Nikolov called 'some idiotic story which people will like'. The keyword in this news discourse is conflict rather than cosmopolitanism, and it is easy to find examples of non-cosmopolitan frames. As Egyptians, Tunisians and Libyans take to the streets, newsreaders tell viewers that 'many' think it is wrong of Europe to send development aid to people toppling their governments, because European governments have needy people at home to be cared for first. There is repeated criticism of interference in the affairs of other countries, and proud reports of Russia upgrading its military forces to meet new threats. When Russia is mentioned, it is either in reports documenting the need for tougher security (against terrorists, for example), or in lighter pieces highlighting a cultural tradition and festivity. The cultural traditions of other countries and regions that might be expected in cosmopolitan accounts figure rarely, if at all.

A rhetorical technique repeatedly drawn on in these strategic narratives is the invocation of 'experts' who are not identified by name or affiliation. With the occasional exception of a university professor, the experts who do appear in person and who are identified by name tend to be outspoken critics of the American and British governments and of 'market forces' (although right-wing populists are also often the primary definers of reports on immigration). The critiques that are levelled at the West are often well-founded. What is 'strategic' about these narratives, and problematic, is that the criticism is always levelled at the US, UK and to a lesser extent Europe, but never Russia, despite the fact that it could also be said that Russia has used international conflicts and unrest in the MidEast to further its own agenda in this period; that Russia also uses imprisonment as a means of controlling political and social unrest; that Russia also lacks the political will to deal with refugee flows and the challenges of multicultural society. While the interviews and news analyses show that Europe is just another part of the interconnected AJE world, it is the Other in the world of RT.

It is not possible to trace strategic narratives in the AJE material explored here. Analysis of its coverage of Egyptian politics from the election of Mohamed Morsi in 2012, through his ousting and the outlawing of the Muslim Brotherhood, to the imprisonment of AJE journalists Peter Greste, Mohamed Fahmy and Baher Mohamed by a Cairo court in 2014 might reveal evidence of them, as might its coverage of the international outrage over treatment of migrant workers in preparations for the 2022 World Cup in Qatar. But the material that has been studied here confirms what journalists and news executives said in the interviews: AJE is a global channel in every sense of the word. It stands out from the others in the comparative analysis of 844 headlines in that the headlines refer to events taking place on every continent. In unfolding crises such as the outbreak of the Arab uprisings, AJE correspondents tended to be part of the story in a way that differed from the other three newsrooms, offering more personal accounts of what they were witnessing and experiencing. AJE had more reporters on the ground than the other channels in the periods studied here, in more places. More of them are locals, and more of them are women.

Between crisis....

One of the analyses reported in Chapter 3 revealed that coding crisis is easier said than done. The distinction between 'crisis' as an issue, on the one hand, and issues framed as crises, on the other, is difficult to maintain in practice. Related to this, the work of documenting the important idea that news reports both communicate and constitute crises (Cottle 2009) poses significant methodological challenges.

As Cottle (2011b, 2009) Hoskins and O'Loughlin (2010) and Philo and Berry (2004) note, there is a need to rethink time-honoured methodological approaches to the analysis of how crisis and dissent are reported. Tidy analytical distinctions between traditional modes of media content, audiences and practices can no longer be maintained, and the interface between these research foci must be treated more dynamically and holistically. Authors such as these argue that there is a need to take into account news media representations of mediality—our relationship to the fact of mediation itself—and to pay attention to how the use of mobile phone and internet technology is represented as part of radicalization processes (Hoskins and O'Loughlin 2010: 189; Grusin 2010). It was in this spirit that Chapter 3 considered the role of social media in television narratives, and depictions of how first-order witnesses connect to each other and the journalists helping them publicize their plight. It transpired that social media do not play the prominent role in global television discourse that they are often ascribed, and that their prominence and deployment varies from one channel to the other. What is 'new' about the new media landscape could be said to have less to do with the technology deployed than on the range of voices and viewpoints with which consumers of television news are invited to connect (although this is obviously not unrelated to technological developments). While it is relatively uncomplicated (if time-consuming) to make note of how television depicts the role of social media, and draws on crowd-sourced material in its own reporting (even if some guesswork is involved), it is less easy to see, document, and make sense of how television itself is becoming transformed in its interaction with these new media forms and practices. The issue of convergence in a discursive sense is arguably the most important one facing media research at present.

When it comes to the 'global' part of 'global crises', the methodological point to be made is its explication warrants considerable attention. The crises referred to in the literature (by Cottle and others) may well be global, but the extent to which they are defined and represented as such by particular newsrooms requires more study. This is of particular interest to work on mediated cosmopolitanism, and of particular political urgency in the context of the framing of economic crisis, as evidenced by the rise of the protectionist right across Europe. Comparative analysis is in order here too: as mentioned at the beginning of this chapter, it reveals that some channels are 'more global' than others. Where RT reporting is reminiscent of the foreign news reporting in the cold-war decades of the 1970s and 80s, its world marked by great power rivalry, AJE reports differently, in a 'new-world-order' sort of way, and it comes the closest to producing the sort of global journalism that Berglez (2013) calls for.

...and cosmopolitanism

The study reported here produced findings that speak against the scepticism expressed by Hafez (2011), who claims that we cannot yet talk of global journalism. As will be recalled from Chapter 1, his conviction is that we can only speak of American, European, or Arab narratives and master frames. This claim turns out to be problematic in two respects. On the one hand, it is too general: leaving aside the Americans and Arabs, there is no common European master-frame, and there is no common narrative of Europe either. On the other hand, the claim is not general enough. From the material analyzed here emerge narratives that are specific to neither a Western nor an Arab context—despite emanating from the Doha-based newsroom—but which can indeed be considered global, in the sense that Cottle (2009) and Berglez (2013) use the term.

The world of AJE is arguably bigger than that of other newsrooms, but it is also smaller. The original managing director, Nigel Parsons, has been quoted as saying in 2005 that the new Al Jazeera channel—just about to start broadcasting in English—would be different because it would treat every news item as a 'foreign story'. What emerges in the interviews conducted with journalists years later suggests that AJE has taken a somewhat different trajectory. Global issues tend instead to be treated as local news. 'We make the local international', as one interviewee put it. 'That's what we do. Really well.'[59]

Another finding was that narratives circulating through global newsrooms like AJE provide more sophisticated imaginative tools than acknowledged by literature on media globalization that focuses on the economic aspects of news production and draws its illustrations from corporate networks like Fox News. Some of the narratives analyzed in Chapters 4 and 5 could be said to belong to Silverstone's mediapolis, in that they provide a space in which we encounter, and are invited to imagine ourselves conversing with, the Other. The tools involved in the construction of such spaces have the potential not only to reduce the distance between, say, Africa and Europe, but also—and perhaps more importantly—to widen our gaze, so we can see the Others who are invisible rather than distant; who are among us, parking our cars, picking our fruit, and cleaning the toilets in the hotels we stay in. The same devices can help us see ourselves as strange. The invitation to travel back with Dennis to the village from which he was abducted as a child, and stand beside him has he steps on the egg in a gesture of reconciliation, is an instance of the perspective-taking involved in the work of the global imagining. Othering, it has been argued, need not always be a negative act, but can be part of that cosmopolitan work. Some news narratives suggest that relationships with the Other are complex and multi-faceted, and can serve as a reminder that the mechanisms of othering should be considered carefully, rather than taken for granted. Empirical research is needed to refine our understanding of how these relationships are established, maintained and perhaps transformed over time and in different cultural and political spaces. There is a fine line between cultural and racial stereotyping, which runs counter to the representation needs of contemporary multicultural societies (be they national or global), and respect for and exploration of difference. This, it could be argued, is the 21st century, societal version of the 'line in the water' between the domestic and foreign that has preoccupied international relations theorists for decades.

The view from the ivory tower and on the ground (theory and practice)

The setting of cosmopolitan connection, to return to the imagery of communicative geography deployed in Chapter 4, has been variously referred to as a global public sphere and as a transnational communicative space. There has been a tendency to emphasize the unifying features of this sphere, including the potential it harbours for shared democratic futures, and the role of the media in propagating common world views and democratic values (Beck 2006). Those who are critical of global television, it has been seen, also emphasize its unifying features.

While not all of them use words like 'oligopoly' and 'electronic colonization', or 'global infotainment', scholars viewing global television from a political economy perspective tend to assume that competition between broadcasters has led to a thinner news diet, an emphasis on trivialization and sensationalism in the pursuit of audience share, and a uniformity of content. As Thussu put it, the 'dominant television news discourse' opts for diversion and 'high-tech infotainment spectacles' rather than 'deeper analysis of geo-political issues' (Thussu 2009a: 132).

Compelling as much of this literature is, the claims it contains are often based on anecdotal evidence from one or a few media (in Thussu's case, those owned by Rupert Murdoch) or the personal impressions of the author veiled in the language of scholarly observation. The output of broadcasters such as those featured in this study is huge, and the landscape of events and problems they report is vast. Claims that television news programmes either encourage viewers to connect with distant others or reduce them to collective stupefaction (Baudrillard 1991/1995) can be easily substantiated by reference to one news report or another. They become more problematic when subjected to comparative analysis. As Cottle (2011a: 78) has lamented, media scholars have yet to do justice to the question of 'how proliferating and interpenetrating global crises are now elaborated and enacted within the complex flows and formations of journalism around the globe'. This book does not do justice to the question either, but it at least provides evidence of the continued need to work on an answer.

Scholars like McPhail are critical of global media that threaten national autonomy, because they pay no heed to geographical boundaries, and influence people's values and perceptions (McPhail 2014: 23). For authors looking out another of the ivory tower's windows, who admire the view over a cosmopolitan landscape, this is precisely as things should be. Global media should be influencing how people perceive the world, so they understand that the important challenges facing them, and the societies of which they are a part, are shared and transgress borders. This is also the view expressed by all the AJE journalists interviewed in this study—people said to earn salaries far beyond the average journalistic wage, but who nevertheless work for a network oblivious to the need for advertising, backed by funders interested in pursuing a soft power agenda rather than profits. While the political economists have important things to say about economic power, and although concerns about what the tyrannies of the advertisement and 'the click' do to quality journalism must always inform any analysis of global media, this preoccupation suffers from (to paraphrase Beck) methodological imperialism. It tends to situate actors such as Murdoch and Fox in the centre of the field of vision, which obscures other institutional and financial solutions to the problem of financing news production. It is imprudent, in global media studies, to discount news channels that are not moored to democracies, especially at a time when democracy itself is best understood as a hybrid (Chadwick 2013).

One of the many questions this study leaves unanswered is about impact. It is difficult to say whether either BBCW's World News, CNNI's International Desk, RT's Journal or AJE's stories of Angola and Uganda do in fact influence how people understand the world. The dual life of these programmes on television and online makes it difficult to make any claims about dissemination—a problem that plagues other research on content and reception in a multi-outlet media landscape.

A related question has to do with how semiotic materials such Surprising Europe, and other documentaries offered by these channels on a variety of platforms, are used. It is reasonable to assume that the availability of 'play' channels online has changed viewer practices in recent years: people now consume series that shape our understanding of identity, society and politics several episodes at a time, or even binge on them, rather than watching installments at weekly intervals—be they *Game of Thrones*, *Homeland* or *Al Jazeera World*. If a series like *Surprising Europe* is engaged with in large portions, the viewer can find herself thinking of the stories of the African narrators continually, and looking at the people of colour in her own European city in a different way. Seeing Europe through the eyes of Ssuuna, Ade, Rose and Sorious means seeing one's own European city through the eyes of others. With a programme like *Surprising Europe* to structure their vision, a person can find the migrants on the streets of Stockholm suddenly taking on brighter hues and coming into much sharper focus as they are passed, while the white Swedes fade and meld into the grey background. There is no empirical evidence to indicate whether this is a typical experience, far less a frequent one, but the othering mechanisms involved are worth further consideration, as is attending to similar texts on offer elsewhere in the globalized mediascape.

Cultural artefacts such as these have considerable potential for the transformative work of the global imagination.

Returning to the global village

Critics of McLuhan's global village point out, on a regular basis, that small communities can be cosy, but are often conformist and consequently tend to be hostile to strangers. How appropriate, then, is the image of the global village to the worlds of the newsrooms visited in this book? And how does it compare to other images of a mediated space beyond national borders, such as Silverstone's mediapolis? What is this place and how much can be learned about it from the analysis of the content of global television news programmes?

If there is still a point in following the news, then there is still a point in doing research on it. An argument has been made here for the continued relevance of analyzing content, and in particular for comparative studies of day-to-day reporting as well as reporting for special occasions (like the Arab uprisings). The worlds of global news are different, and the temptation should be resisted to make unhelpful generalizations. Through comparative analysis, the differences in narrative strategies become apparent, and those differences provide the basis for thinking about the challenges of representation in societies whose politics and economies are becoming increasingly intermeshed, but whose disaffected have shown an inclination to withdraw from collective solutions and cultural integration.

Said's project was to show how the Orient was a European invention that helped define Europe in a discursive process of hetero-identification. One of the two imperial narratives he discerned was of powerful (and superior) Westerners imposing order (and themselves) on the jungle and its inhabitants. What if the jungle is a world that is increasingly interconnected, and increasingly burdened by problems that transcend national borders—a vortex of issues and actors rather than one characterized by a neat distinction between 'domestic' and 'foreign' news? Who is understood as imposing order; who are 'we', and who are 'the Rest'? If the focus is not on the informative content of news broadcasts, but on the function of the narratives that convey that information, is there 're-orientation' in evidence?

To answer such questions, attention must be paid to the more instrumental function of news narratives that speak to global audiences. More than half a century ago, in a world divided by the Cold War, Boulding argued that the unsophisticated image sees the world only from one viewpoint, while 'the sophisticated image sees the world from many imagined viewpoints, as a system in which the viewer is only a part'. The horizon of the person who sees the world through the eyes of others 'extends to other times, places and cultures than his own' (Boulding 1959: 130). Many wars later, the take-home message is that there are narrative techniques at work in the global newsroom, albeit more in some corners than others, that produce the sophisticated images Boulding had in mind. The perspective-taking they offer is a challenge to viewer and researcher alike, and give cause to rethink 'othering' as something inevitably negative. It can in practice be multi-dimensional and polysemic, and conducive to the representations of difference which can be thought to nourish cosmopolitan outlooks.

Sophistication and high-quality reporting is often assumed—particularly in the scholarly literature—to involve informative accounts of issues and processes. This is what Berglez seems to have in mind when calling for a new 'global journalist' approach. 'Personalization' strategies are looked down on in much of the literature on political communication: they trivialize; they are human interest gimmicks designed to 'wheedle attention' from a mildly literate audience, as Rosenblum put it. Another possibility has been suggested here. Putting people in the centre of news narratives may not be pandering to consumers suffering from attention deficits or the cause of superficial accounts of complex globalization processes. They can be seen as serving the opposite purpose—offering the journalistic equivalent of thick description, the possibility of Verstehen, and of seeing the world through many different eyes. Viewers may include not only the mildly literate, but the illiterate, when the aim is to reach a global audience. For some journalists in the global newsroom—referred to elsewhere (Robertson 2010) as workers of the global imagination that is not a problem, that is the point.

The sort of analyses presented in this book cannot stand on their own. There is a need to contextualize them, and the scholarly discussions they enable, by mapping connectivity in the larger narratives of which news broadcasts are comprised. We need to compare who different broadcasters entrust with the task of conveying the testimony of the people in the worlds constituted by global news discourse. We need to look to see whose eyes events unfold through, and listen to who is describing them. We need to pay attention to whether the spectator is placed in a dialogic situation vis-a-vis the witness and perhaps even called on to participate, even if vicariously. As Benhabib and Tomlinson have observed, the blogosphere creates one kind of conversation, but democracy, particularly in a globalizing world, is not just about exchanging views and opinions: it is also about dialogue on learning to live together in the 'cultural chaos' of contemporary media connectivity (Tomlinson 2011: 360). Television remains a key player in this regard.

This book has had something else in its sights than businessmen consuming media such as *Time*, *Newsweek* and *The Economist* in a global society that does not include the Middle East and Africa, as sketched by Hachten & Scotton (2011) in the eighth edition of the *World News Prism*. The central concept throughout has been not 'international', 'transnational' or 'foreign' news, but global news. The intention has been to sort through and juxtapose competing claims in the literature on this topic, and evaluate them in the light of unusual empirical evidence. It is, arguably, necessary work given that key disagreements in the study of global media flows can be traced back to a lack of conceptual rigour, the choice of empirical evidence (to the extent that evidence rather than anecdotes is brought to the scholarly table) and, not least, which window the inhabitants of the ivory tower look out of, when surveying the contours of the global media landscape.

With technological advances, a world is made available to us in ways that were previously unimaginable. But that world is plural, according to Silverstone: the world as it appears on Al Arabya is different from that on CNN. 'The public space which reflects, expresses, as well as distorts the appearance of the global on the screens of both broadcast and on-line media is a contested space', he argues, dismissing as absurd the presumption that global mediated culture is homogenous (Silverstone 2007: 6, 12). In exploring what happens in this space, then, the researcher should take care not to stay put in one world, but to move between different ones—not just that of CNN International but also of Russia Today; not just that BBC World but also of Al Jazeera English. There is a world of difference between them.

NOTES

1. Interview in Doha, September 2012, with Ramsay Zarifeh, Executive Producer, Al Jazeera.
2. http://advertising.bbcworldwide.com/home/mediakit/reachaudience/bbcworldnews. BBC World News reached 285 million homes in 2009 and estimated its audience as 78 million viewers weekly. Dencik (2013: 7) reports that in terms of both reach and audience it is predominantly European, with 'large stakes' in the Middle East and Asia. Its US audience has grown steadily since the Iraq War of 2003.
3. http://cnnpressroom.blogs.cnn.com/cnn-fact-sheet/
4. http://www.aljazeera.com/aboutus/
5. http://rt.com/about-us/distribution/; interview with Alina Mikhaleva, Head of RT's Media & External Communications Department.
6. RT correspondent Anastasia Churkina, reporting from New York, 29 January 2011.
7. The first is Steve Randall, senior analyst of FAIR, a not uncontroversial media monitoring group that keeps close tabs on the US right but which has been accused by Beth Gilinsky, president of the Jewish Action Alliance, of ignoring racist and anti-Semitic broadcasts on radio stations targetting black audiences, and by Tim Graham of the Media Research Center in Alexandria, Virginia of reiterating the same arguments, without requiring or producing evidence for them. The second is Danny Schechter, billed on this item as 'Media Critic'. Schechter is a journalist, author and filmmaker who at the time of the broadcast was working for AJE. The third, billed as 'Media Analyst', is T.J. Walker, a media trainer appearing on Bloomberg TV, The Daily Show and Fox News and the fourth a Georgetown University professor, Chris Chambers. The fifth expert interviewed in this piece is Laura Flanders, billed as 'Broadcaster and Author', who describes herself as a

'liberal, lefty person' who at the time of the broadcast presented the GRITtv programme, broadcast on FreeSpeech TV.

8. Head of News London/Executive Producer Al Jazeera English Ben Rayner. One of the correspondents put it more forcefully. 'The Saudis may have got most of the oil, bought a lot of gold, but the Emir of Qatar changed the course of history', said Middle East correspondent Anita McNaught. 'It is just amazing what the impact of bringing free speech to the Middle East has had, the Middle East was revolutionized, galvanized, electrified by it. I think the guy's a genius. It might have been an accidental brainstorm to start of with, but at least he followed it through, he was committed to it. It became a foreign policy tool for a country of 200 thousand people, that now punches well above it's weight, how and why does it do that? Because of Al Jazeera.'
9. http://www.foxnews.com/world/2012/04/17/wikileaks-founder-show-to-air-on-kremlin-tv/
10. http://eng.kremlin.ru/news/5571
11. 'About Al Jazeera English', booklet available to visitors to the newsroom, no author or date.
12. They are in:
Sub Saharan Africa: Abuja (Nigeria), Harare (Zimbabwe), Johannesburg (South Africa), Nairobi (Kenya), Ndjamena (Chad).
Asia: Bangkok (Thailand), Beijing (China), Delhi (India), Jakarta (Indonesia), Kuala Lumpur (Malaysia), Manila (Philippines), Seoul (South Korea), Sydney (Australia), Tokyo (Japan).
North Africa: Casablanca (Morocco), Khartoum (Sudan), Nouakchott (Mauritania), Mogadishu (Somalia), Tripoli (Libya), Tuni (Tunisia).
Americas: Buenos Aires (Argentina), Chicago (US), Los Angeles (US), Mexico City (Mexico), Miami, New York, Sao Paulo (Brazil), Toronto, Washington.
Europe: Ankara (turkey), Belgrade (Serbia), Berlin (Germany), Brussels (Belgium), Istanbul (Turkey), London, Madrid, Moscow, Oslo, Paris, Sarajevo (Bosnia), Skopje (Macedonia), Zagreb (Croatia).
Middle East: Amman (Jordan), Arbil (Iraq), Baghdad (Iraq), Beirut (Lebanon), Caito, Damascas (Syria), Dubai (UAE), Gaza (Palestine), Islamabad (Pakistan), Jeddah (Saudi Arabia), Jerusalem (no country), Kabul (Afghanistan), Kuwait (Kuwait), Muscat (Oman), Ramallah (Palestine), Riyadh (Saudi Arabia), Sana (Yemen), Tehran (Iran).
13. In 2012, awards included: Royal Television Society, News Channel for the Year, 2012.
Royal Television Society, Most Innovative Programme (the Stream), 2012.
The Franklin D. Roosevelt Four Freedoms Awards, Freedom of Speech and Expression Medal 2012; Amnesty International Media Award and Monte Carlo TV Festival, Golden Nymph for Best News documentary for *Bahrain: Shouting in the Dark*; and the
Peabody Award. In 2013, it won, among other prizes, four CINE Golden Eagle Awards for its investigative journalism, two Human Rights Press Awards, two Foreign Press Association awards and an Asia TV Award. By midway through 2014, it had won the Women's Empowerment Journalism Awards Broadcast Story Of The Year, two George Foster Peabody awards and won the highest number of prizes at the Hong Kong Human Rights Awards.
14. http://www.aljazeera.com/aboutus/2006/11/2008525185733692771.html

15. Ramsay Zarifeh, Executive Producer, Doha.
16. Carlos van Meek, Head of Current Affairs, Doha.
17. Mohammed Adow, Doha-based roving correspondent, with 15 years' experience of reporting from Africa.
18. Mohammed Adow, roving and Africa correspondent, and Head of Current Affairs Carlos van Meek.
19. Ben Rayner, Head of News London/Executive Producer.
20. Will Thorne, Executive Producer of News in Doha (Acting Head of Online at the time of the interview).
21. Ramsay Zarifeh, Executive Producer.
22. Anita McNaught, Middle East Correspondent.
23. Omar Alsaleh, Senior Producer and Reporter.
24. Doha newsreader Adrian Finighan.
25. Ramsay Zarifeh, Executive Producer, Doha.
26. Ben Rayner, Head of News London/Executive Producer.
27. Will Thorne, Acting Head of Online.
28. Adrian Finighan, newsreader, Doha.
29. Salah Negem, Director of News.
30. Ben Rayner, Head of News London/Executive Producer.
31. Anita McNaught, Middle East Correspondent.
32. Anita McNaught, Middle East Correspondent.
33. Anita McNaught, Middle East Correspondent.
34. Mohammed Adow, Doha-based roving correspondent, with 15 years' experience of reporting from Africa.
35. Anita McNaught, Middle East Correspondent.
36. AJE Middle East correspondent Anita McNaught, interviewed in Doha in September 2012.
37. The BBC programme analysed here is BBC World News, broadcast at 10 pm CET. For CNN, International Desk has been used. It is broadcast at 7pm CET (replaced, on occasion—holidays, for example—by World Report. For RT, the 7pm CET broadcast has been coded. The AJE sample varies, as the advertised broadcast was not always what appeared on screen in the period coded here (especially January 2011). The intention was to code the 30-minute broadcast anchored from London, broadcast at 8pm CET. Instead of this, the 8pm broadcast was sometimes the 60-minute Newshour from Doha (anchored from London in 2013 as well). The differing lengths of the programmes have been taken into account in calculations presented later on in the chapter.
38. For technical reasons, the CNNI sample includes only 18 broadcasts, and 2 programmes are missing from the AJE 2012 sample. The AJE sample includes two different programmes because the 30 minute News from London, selected as the unit of analysis for various reasons,5 was often replaced by a 60-minute Newshour, without warning. This was especially the case during the tumultuous weeks between the posting of Bouazizi's self-immolation on Facebook and the ousting of Egyptian president Mubarak.
39. The other items using amateur video were about the floods in Australia and the bombing at Moscow airport.

40. The other items were about a Russian company's investment in Facebook, and a YouTube video posted by a girl in Yellowknife of boiling water that froze upon hitting the winter air. As Yellowknife is in the far north of Canada, the point of the story can safely be assumed to be the fact that her 30 second clip went viral.
41. One of these occasions was the bombing of Moscow airport.
42. On one of these, it was reported that the US was taking legal action to gain access to Twitter accounts involved in recent WikiLeaks disclosures, and one was a business item about the internet site Myspace laying off employees, due to competition from Facebook.
43. Four others were about the Moscow airport bomb and one about how Americans celebrate divorces these days, and not just weddings.
44. 'Colour Revolution Failures Cloud Future of North Africa Protest Wave', RT, 28 January 2011.
45. This is not to suggest that protesters and Al Jazeera always saw eye-to-eye: in another city on this day, an AJ satellite truck was set alight by demonstrators.
46. Anita McNaught, op.cit.
47. Ben Rayner, Executive Producer, Al Jazeera English, interviewed in London in June 2013.
48. Carlos van Meek, Head of Current Affairs at AJE, interviewed in Doha in 2012.
49. Salah Negem, News Director, AJE Doha, interviewed in Doha in 2012.
50. Ramsay Zarifeh, Executive Producer at AJE, interviewed in Doha in 2012.
51. Ben Rayner, op. cit.
52. Harvey, D. (2009) *Social Justice and the City*. Athens, GA: University of Georgia Press.
53. Bourdon 2007: 266.
54. http://www.aljazeera.com/programmes/surprisingeurope/, accessed 17 July 2014.
55. Ben Rayner, Executive Producer, Al Jazeera English, interviewed in London in June 2013.
56. Ben Rayner, Executive Producer, Al Jazeera English, interviewed in London in June 2013.
57. The first programme of the week was broadcast at 22:30 GMT and repeated the following morning, in the middle of the following European night (Wednesday 03:30) and Thursday afternoon (16:30 GMT). It could still be viewed online at http://www.aljazeera.com/programmes/surprisingeurope/ in October 2012.
58. Anita McNaught, correspondent. That said, BBC World has some 'exceptionally good' women covering the news: the work of Lyse Doucet is highly praised by the AJE correspondent quoted above, and stands out in reporting studied here and elsewhere (Robertson 2010).
59. Carlos van Meek.

REFERENCES

Adams, P.C. & Jansson, A. (2012) 'Communication geography: A bridge between disciplines', *Communication Theory 22* (3): 299–318.

Aiello, G. (2011) 'The "other" Europeans: the semiotic imperative of style in Euro Visions by Magnum Photos', *Visual Communication 11* (1). 49–77.

Al Jazeera (2013a) 'Al Jazeera buys US channel Current TV', 3 January, http://www.aljazeera.com/news/americas/2013/01/201313225576913O.html, accessed 3 January 2013.

Al Jazeera English (2010a) "Corporate Profile", http://english.aljazeera.net/aboutus/2006/11/2008525185555444449.html, accessed 9/3/11.

Al Jazeera English (2010b) "Code of Ethics", http://english.aljazeera.net/aboutus/2006/11/2008525185733692771.html, accessed 9/3/11.

Al-Sadi, M. (2012) 'Al Jazeera Television: Rhetoric of Deflection', *Arab Media & Society*, Issue 15, www.arabmediasociety.com/?article=786, accessed 8 July 2012.

Andén-Papadopoulos, K. & Pantti, M., eds. (2011) *Amateur Images & Global News*. Intellect Books.

Anderson, Nate (2011) "Tweeting tyrants out of Tunisia: the global internet at its best", Ars Technica January 15th, http://arstechnica.com, accessed 21/01/11.

Appadurai, A. (1996) *Modernity at Large: Cultural Dimensions of Globalization*. London: University of Minnesota Press.

Appadurai, A. (1990) 'Disjuncture and Difference in the Global Cultural Economy', in M. Featherstone, ed., *Global Culture: Nationalism, Globalization and Modernity*. London: Sage.

Appiah, K.A. (2001) 'Cosmopolitan Reading', in Dharwadker, V., ed. *Cosmopolitan Geographies. New Locations in Literature and Culture*. New York & London: Routledge.

Arceneaux, N. & Schmitz Weiss, A. (2010) 'Seems stupid until you try it: press coverage of Twitter, 2006–9', *New Media & Society* 12(8): 1262–1279.

Archetti, C. (2008) 'News coverage of 9/11 and the demise of the media flows, globalization and localization hypotheses', *The International Communication Gazette 70* (6): 463–485.

Ashuri, T. (2006) "Television tension: national versus cosmopolitan memory in a co-produced television documentary". *Media, Culture and Society 29* (1): 31–51.

Ashuri, T. & Pinchevski, A. (2009) 'Witnessing as a Field', in Frosh, P. & Pinchevsky, A., eds. *Media Witnessing. Testimony in the Age of Mass Communication*. London: Palgrave Macmillan.

Auter, P.J., Arafa, M. & Al-Jaber, K. (2005) 'Identifying with Arabic Journalists. How Al-Jazeera Tapped Parasocial Interaction Gratifications in the Arab World', *Gazette: The International Journal for Communication Studies* 67(2): 189–204.

Azran, T. (2004) 'Resisting Peripheral Exports: Al Jazeera's War Images on US Television', *Media International Australia 113*: 75–86.

Bahry, L.Y. (2001) 'The New Arab Media Phenomenon: Qatar's Al-Jazeera', *Middle East Policy* 8 (2): 88–99.

Balibar, E. (2012) 'Citizenship of the World Revisited', in Delanty, G., ed. *Routledge Handbook of Cosmopolitan Studies*. London: Routledge, pp. 291–301.

Barakat, R. (2011) New media in the Arab World: A tool for redesigning geopolitical realities. Masters thesis, Lebanese American University, https://ecommons.lau.edu.lb:8443/xmlui/handle/10725/1047?show=full.

Barker, C. (1999) *Television, Globalization and Cultural Identities*. Buckingham: Open University Press.

Barnhurst, K.G. (2011) 'The New Media "Affect" and the Crisis of Representation for Political Communication', *International Journal of Press/Politics 16* (4): 573–593.

Barthes, R. (1993 [1957]) *Mythologies*. London: Vintage.

Baudrillard, J. (1991/1995) The Gulf War Did Not Take Place. Bloomington: Indiana University Press.

Bauman, Z. (1991) *Modernity and Ambivalence*. Cambridge: Polity.

BBC (2011) "Libya: Gaddafi forces detain and beat BBC Arabic team", March 10th, www.bbc.co.uk/news/world-africa-12695077, accessed 10/03/11.

Beaumont, P. (2012) 'Europe's new insurgents: rising rebels spurn the era of bling', The Observer, 20 May, http://www.theguardian.com/world/2012/may/20/europe-new-leaders-generation-normal, accessed 15 September.

Beck, U. (2006) *Cosmopolitan Vision*. Cambridge: Polity.

Beck, U. (2012) 'Global inequality and human rights: a cosmopolitan perspective', in Delanty, G., ed. *Routledge Handbook of Cosmopolitan Studies*. London: Routledge, pp. 302–315.

Beck, U. & Levy, D. (2013) 'Cosmopolitanized Nations: Re-imagining Collectivity in World Risk Society', *Theory, Culture & Society* 30 (2): 3–31.

Becker, K. (2012) 'Performing Photograph—Performing the News'. Paper presented at the PhotoMedia conference in Helsinki, 28–30 March.

Belo, A. et al. (2013) 'Actors in Foreign News', in Cohen, A.A., ed. *Foreign News on Television. Where in the World Is the Global Village?* New York: Peter Lang, pp. 87–105.

Bennett, L.W. (2003) 'New Media Power: the Internet and Global Activism', in N. Couldry & J. Curran, eds. *Contesting Media Power: Alternative Media in a Networked World.* Oxford: Rowman & Littlefield.

Bennett, W. L. & Segerberg, A. (2012) 'The Logic of Connective Action. Digital media and the personalization of contentious politics', *Information, Communication & Society 15* (5): 739–768.

Berger, G. (2009) 'How the Internet Impacts on International News. Exploring Paradoxes of the Most Global Medium in a Time of "Hyperlocalism"', *The International Communication Gazette 71*(5): 355–371.

Berglez, P. (2013) *Global Journalism. Theory and Practice.* New York: Peter Lang.

Berglez, P. (2008) 'What Is Global Journalism? Theoretical and Empirical Conceptualisations. *Journalism Studies* 9 (6): 845–858.

Bhabha, H. (2004) *The Location of Culture.* Abingdon: Routledge.

Bhabha, H. (1990) *Nation and Narration.* London: Routledge.

Bimber, B. (2012) 'Digital Media and Citizenship' in Semetko, H. & Scammell, M. (eds) *The Sage Handbook of Political Communication.* London: Sage, pp. 115–126).

Birkvad, S. (2000) 'A Battle for Public Mythology: History and Genre in the Portrait Documentary', *Nordicom Review 21* (2): 291–304.

Bjerström. E. (2013) *Det Nya Afrika.* Stockholm: Weyler.

Bloomfield, S. (2014) 'Ofcom Should Be Looking Again at Putin's TV News Channel', *The Guardian*, 24 April.

Bolling, A. (2013) 'Världen bättre än vad du tror', Dagens Nyheter, 26 October, http://www.dn.se/goda-nyheter/varlden-battre-an-vad-du-tror/, accessed 26 October 2013.

Boltanski, L. (1999) *Distant Suffering: Morality, Media and Politics.* Cambridge: Cambridge University Press.

Borger, J. (2012) 'Ratko Mladic goes on trial for Bosnian war crimes', The Guardian, 16 May, http://www.theguardian.com/world/2012/may/16/ratko-mladic-trial-bosnia-war-crimes.

Boulding, K. (1959) 'National Images and International Systems', *Conflict Resolution 3* (2): 120–31.

Bourdieu, P. (1999) *On Television.* New York: The New Press.

Bourdieu, P. (1993) *The Field of Cultural Production.* Cambridge: Polity.

Bourdon, J. (2007) 'Unhappy Engineers of the European Soul: The EBU and the Woes of Pan European Television', *International Communication Gazette* 69 (3): 263–280).

Boyd-Barrett, O. (2009) 'Changing Paradigms of Media Research and Practice in Contexts of Globalization and Terror', in Thussu, D.K., ed. *Internationalizing Media Studies.* London: Routledge, pp. 116–130.

Boyd-Barrett, O. (2007) 'Alternative Reframing of Mainstream Media Frames', in Thussu, D.K., ed. *Media on the Move. Global Flow and Contra-flow.* London: Routledge, pp. 201–220.

Boyd-Barrett, O. & Rantanen, T., eds. (1998) *The Globalization of News*. London: Sage.

Brüggemann, M. & Kleinen-von Königslöw, K. (2009) '"Let's Talk about Europe". Why Europeanization Shows a Different Face in Different Newspapers', *European Journal of Communication 24* (1): 27–48.

Brüggemann, M. & Schulz-Forberg, H. (2009) 'Becoming Pan-European? Transnational Media and the European Public Sphere', *The International Communication Gazette 71* (8): 693–712.

Bruner, J. (1991) 'The Narrative Construction of Reality', *Critical Inquiry 18*: 1–21.

Calhoun, C. (2004) 'A World of Emergencies: Fear, Intervention, and the Limits of Cosmopolitan Order', *Canadian Review of Sociology/Revue canadienne de sociologie*, *41* (4): 373–395.

Caquard, S. (2011) 'Cartography I: Mapping Narrative Cartography', *Progress in Human Geography 37* (1): 135–144.

Castells, M. (2009) *Communication Power*. Oxford: Oxford University Press.

Césaire, A. (2000) *Discourse on Colonialism*. New York: Monthly Review Press.

Chadwick, A. (2013) *The Hybrid Media System. Politics and Power*. Oxford: Oxford University Press.

Chan, J.M. & Lee, F.L.F. (2013) 'Foreign News on Public and Commercial Stations', in Cohen, A.A., ed. *Foreign News on Television. Where in the World Is the Global Village?* New York: Peter Lang, pp. 129–150.

Chang, T-K. (1998) 'All Countries Not Created Equal to Be News. World System and International Communication', *Communication Research 25* (5): 528–563.

Chang, T-K., Southwell, B., Lee, H-M & Hong, Y. (2000) 'A Changing World, Unchanging Perspectives: American Newspaper Editorials and Enduring Values in Foreign News Reporting', *The International Communication Gazette 74* (4): 367–384.

Charles, J., Shore, L. & Todd, R. (1979) '*The New York Times* Coverage of Equatorial and Lower Africa', *Journal of Communication 29* (2): 148–155.

Chatman, S. (1978) *Story and Discourse: Narrative Structure in Fiction and Film*. Ithaca, N.Y. & London: Cornell University Press.

Cheah, P. (2013) '"The World Is Watching". The Mediatic Structure of Cosmopolitanism', *Journalism Studies 14* (2): 219–231.

Cheah, P. (2012) 'What Is a World? On World Literature as World-making Activity', in Delanty, G., ed. *Routledge Handbook of Cosmopolitan Studies*. London: Routledge, pp. 138–149.

Chernilo, D. (2012) 'Cosmopolitanism and the Question of Universalism', in Delanty, G., ed. *Routledge Handbook of Cosmopolitan Studies*. London: Routledge, pp. 47–59.

Chevaldonné, F. (1987) 'Globalization and Orientalism—the Case of TV Serials', *Media, Culture & Society* 9 (2): 137–48.

Chopra, R. & Gajjala, R., eds. (2011) *Global Media, Culture, and Identity. Theory, Cases and Approaches*. Abingdon: Routledge.

Chouliaraki, L. (2006) *The Spectatorship of Suffering*. London: Sage.

Chouliaraki, L. (2008) 'The Symbolic Power of Transnational Media', *Global Media and Communication* 4: 329–51

Chouliaraki, L. (2010a) 'Post-humanitarianism. Humanitarian Communication Beyond a Politics of Pity', *International Journal of Cultural Studies 13* (2): 107–126.

Chouliaraki, L. (2010b) 'Ordinary Witnessing in Post-television News: Toward a New Moral Imagination', *Critical Discourse Studies 7* (3): 305–19.

Chouliaraki, L. (2013) 'Re-mediation, Inter-mediation, Trans-mediation', *Journalism Studies* ISSN 1461–670X.

Chouliaraki, L. & Blaagaard, B. (2013) 'Introduction: Cosmopolitanism and the New News Media', *Journalism Studies 14* (2): 150–155.

Christensen, M., Jansson, A., & Christensen, C., eds. (2011) *Online Territories: Globalization, Mediated Practice and Social Space*. New York and London: Peter Lang.

Clark, A.M. & Werder, O. (2007) 'Analyzing International Radio Stations. A Systems Approach', *The International Communications Gazette* 69 (6): 525–537.

Clausen, L. (2004) 'Localizing the Global: "Domestication" Processes in International News Production', *Media, Culture and Society 26* (1): 25–44.

Clausen, L. (2003) *Global News Production*. Copenhagen: Copenhagen Business School.

Cobley, P. (2014) *Narrative*, second edition. London: Routledge.

Cohen, A.A. (2013) 'Where in the World Is the Global Village?', in Cohen, A.A., ed. *Foreign News on Television. Where in the World Is the Global Village?* New York: Peter Lang, pp. 319–330.

Cohen, A. et al. (1996) *Global Newsrooms, Local Audiences: A Study of the Eurovision News Exchange*. London: John Libbey.

Cohen, A. et al. (2013) 'Rationale, Design, and Methodologies', in Cohen, A.A., ed. *Foreign News on Television. Where in the World Is the Global Village?* New York: Peter Lang, pp. 3–22.

Committee to Protect Journalists (2011a) "CPJ condemns attacks on press in Libya, Yemen and Egypt", March 9th, www.cpj.org/2011/03/cpj-condemns-attacks-on-press-in-libya-yemen-and-e.php, accessed 10/03/11

Committee to Protect Journalists (2011b) "Tunisia must end censorship on coverage of unrest", open letter to President Zine Abidine Ben Ali, January 5th, www.cpj.org/2011/01/tunisia-must-end-censorship-on-coverage-of-unrest.php, accessed 10/01/11.

Conway, K. (2010) 'Paradoxes of Translation in Television news', *Media, Culture & Society 32* (6): 979–996.

Cottle, S. (2006) *Mediatized Conflict*. Maidenhead: Open University Press.

Cottle, S. (2008) 'Reporting Demonstrations: The Changing Media Politics of Dissent', *Media, Culture & Society* 30 (6): 853–872.

Cottle, S. (2009) *Global Crisis Reporting. Journalism in the Global Age*. Maidenhead: Open University Press.

Cottle, S. (2011a) 'Taking Global Crises in the News Seriously: Notes from the Dark Side of Globalization', *Global Media and Communication 7* (2): 77–95.

Cottle, S. (2011b) 'Media and the Arab Uprisings of 2011: Research Notes', *Journalism 12* (5): 647–659.

Cottle, S. (2011c) 'Transnational Protests and the Media: New Departures, Challenging Debates', in Cottle, S. & Lester, L. eds., *Transnational Protests and the Media*. New York: Peter Lang.

Cottle, S. (2011d) 'Cell Phones, Camels and the Global Call for Democracy', http://www.opendemocracy.net/simon-cottle/cell-phones-camels-and-global-call-for-democracy, 27 September.

Cottle, S. & Rai, M. (2008a) 'Television News in India: Mediating Democracy and Difference', *The International Communication Gazette* 70 (1): 76–96.

Cottle, S. & Rai, M. (2008b) 'Television News in South Africa: Mediating an Emerging Democracy', *Journal of Southern African Studies* 34 (2): 343–358.

Cottle, S. & and Rai, M. (2008c) "Global 24/7 News Providers. Emissaries of Global Dominance or Global Public Service?" *Global Media and Communication* 4 (2): 157–181.

Couldry, N. (2010) *Why Voice Matters; Culture and Politics after Neoliberalism*. London: Sage.

Couldry, N. (2008) 'Mediatization or Mediation? Alternative Understandings of the Emergent Space of Digital Storytelling', *New Media & Society* 10 (3): 373–391.

Couldry, N., Hepp, A. & Krotz, F. (2010) *Media Events in a Global Age*. Abingdon and New York: Routledge.

Curtin, M. (2010) 'Comparing Media Capitals: Hong Kong and Mumbai', *Global Media and Communication* 6 (3): 263–270.

Czarniawska, B. (2004) *Narratives in Social Science Research*. London: Sage.

D'Haenens, L. & Verelst, C. (2002) 'Portrayal of Indonesia's Reform in the Dutch Print Media', International Communication Gazette 64(2): 183–97.

Dahlberg, L. & Siapera, E. (2007) *Radical Democracy and the Internet*. Houndmills: Palgrave.

Dayan, D. (2010) 'Beyond Media Events. Disenchantment, Derailment, Disruption', in Couldry, N. et al. eds., *Media Events in a Global Age*. Abingdon and New York: Routledge.

Dayan, Daniel and Elihu Katz (1992) *Media Events. The Live Broadcasting of History*. Cambridge and London: Harvard University Press.

De Beer, A. S. (2004) 'News—The Fleeting, Elusive but Essential Feature of Global Journalism', in de Beer, A. & Merrill, J.C., eds., *Global Journalism. Topical Issues and Media Systems*. Boston: Pearson, pp. 163–177.

De Kloet, J. (2013) 'Europe as Façade', *European Journal of Cultural Studies* 17 (1). 58–74.

De Swert, K. et al. (2013) 'Topics in Foreign and Domestic Television News', in Cohen, A.A., ed. *Foreign News on Television. Where in the World Is the Global Village?* New York: Peter Lang, pp. 41–62.

Delanty, G. (2006) 'The Cosmopolitan Imagination: Critical Cosmopolitanism and Social Theory', *British Journal of Sociology* 57 (1): 25–47.

Delanty, G. (2012) 'The Idea of Critical Cosmopolitanism', in Delanty, G., ed. *Routledge Handbook of Cosmopolitan Studies*. London: Routledge, pp. 38–46.

Deluca, K.M. & Peeples, J. (2002) 'From Public Sphere to Public Screen: Democracy, Activism, and the "Violence" of Seattle', *Critical Studies in Media Communication* 19 (2): 125–151

Dencik, L. (2011) *Media and Global Civil Society*. Basingstoke: Palgrave Macmillan.

Dencik, L. (2013) 'What Global Citizens and Whose Global Moral Order? Defining the Global at BBC World News', *Global Media and Communication* 9 (2): 1–16.

Deuze, M. (2004) 'Global Journalism Education', in de Beer, A. & Merrill, J.C., eds., *Global Journalism. Topical Issues and Media Systems*. Boston: Pearson, pp. 128–141.

Dharwadker, V., ed. (2001) *Cosmopolitan Geographies. New Locations in Literature and Culture.* New York & London: Routledge.

Dong, S.G. & Shi, A. (2007) 'Chinese News in Transition: Facing the Challenge of Global Competition', in Thussu, D.K., ed. *Media on the Move. Global Flow and Contra-flow.* London: Routledge, pp. 182–197.

Donk, W. et al., eds. (2004) *Cyberprotest: New Media, Citizens and Social Movements*. Chicago: University of Chicago Press.

Dyer, R. (1977) 'Stereotyping', in Dyer, R. ed., *Gays and Film*. London: British Film Institute.

Dzyadko, T. (2014) 'Triumph of the Will: Putin's War Against Russia's Last Independent TV Channel', *The Guardian*, April 10th.

Ekecrantz, J. (2009) 'Media and Communication Studies Going Global', in Thussu, D.K., ed. *Internationalizing Media Studies*. London: Routledge, pp. 75–89.

Ekström, A. (2012) 'Exhibiting Disasters: Mediation, Historicity and Spectatorship', *Media, Culture & Society 34* (4): 472–487.

El-Ibiary, R. (2011) 'Questioning the Al-Jazeera Effect: Analysis of Al-Qaeda's Media Strategy and Its Relationship with Al-Jazeera', *Global Media and Communication 7* (3): 199–204.

Ellis, John (2009) "Mundane Witness" in Paul Frosch and Amit Pinchchevsky, eds., *Media Witnessing. Testimony in the Age of Mass Communication*. Houndmills: Palgrave Macmillan, pp. 73–88.

el-Nawawy, M. & Iskander, A. (2003) *Al-Jazeera*. Cambridge, MA: Westview Press.

el-Nawawy, M. & Powers, S. (2010) 'Al-Jazeera English. A Conciliatory Medium in a Conflict-driven Environment?' *Global Media and Communication* 6 (1): 61–84.

Eurodata (2014) 'One Television Year in the World', http://www.mediametrie.com/eurodatatv/solutions/one-television-year-in-the-world.php?id=57, accessed 9 October 2014.

European Federation of Journalists (2012) 'European jobs crisis damaging journalism: EFJ stands in support of ETUC day of action', http://europe.ifj.org/en/articles/european-jobs-crisis-damaging-journalism-efj-stands-in-support-of-etuc-day-of-action, accessed 17 November 2012.

Fahmy, S.S. & Al Emad, M. (2011) 'Al-Jazeera vs Al-Jazeera: A Comparison of the Network's English and Arabic Online Coverage of the US/Al Qaeda Conflict', *The International Communication Gazette 73* (3): 216–232.

Figenschou, T.U. (2010) 'A Voice for the Voiceless? A Quantitative Content Analysis of Al-Jazeera English's Flagship News', *Global Media and Communication* 6 (1): 85–107.

Figenschou, T.U. (2011) 'Suffering Up Close: The Strategic Construction of Mediated Suffering on Al Jazeera English', *International Journal of Communication* 5: 233–253.

Figenschou, T. (2012) 'The South Is Talking back: With a White Face and a British Accent—Editorial Dilemmas in Al Jazeera English', *Journalism: Theory, Practice & Criticism 13* (3): 354–370.

Figenschou, T. (2013) *Al Jazeera and the Global Media Landscape: The South Is Talking Back.* New York: Routledge.

Fine, R. (2012) 'The Idea of Cosmopolitan Solidarity', in Delanty, G., ed. *Routledge Handbook of Cosmopolitan Studies.* London: Routledge, pp. 376–386.

Firmstone, J. (2008) 'Approaches of the Transnational Press to Reporting Europe', *Journalism* 9 (4): 423–442.

Flew, T. (2007) *Understanding Global Media.* Basingstoke: Palgrave Macmillan.

Franklin, B. (2005) 'The Local Press and the McDonaldization Thesis', in Allan, S. ed. *Journalism: Critical Issues.* New York: McGraw-Hill International.

Freeman, B.C. (2010) 'Through a Western Lens. Portrayals of a "Rising" ASEAN and Its Member Countries in *The New York Times*', *The International Communication Gazette* 72 (3): 269–285.

Freemantle, J. (2011) 'The day my boss held a Kalashnikov to my head', http://jamesfreemantle.com/the-day-my-boss-held-a-kalashnikov-to-my-head/, accessed 9 January 2011.

Frosh, P. (2011) 'Phatic Morality: Television and Proper Distance', *International Journal of Cultural Studies 14* (4): 383–400.

Frosh, P. & Pinchevsky, A. (2009) *Media Witnessing. Testimony in the Age of Mass Communication.* Houndmills: Palgrave Macmillan.

Fuchs, C. (2010) 'New Imperialism. Information and Media Imperialism?', *Global Media and Communication* 6 (1): 33–60.

Gahran, Amy (2011) "How Al Jazeera is putting audio updates from Egypt online fast", Knight Digital Media Center, www.knightdigitalmediacenter.org, accessed 14/02/11.

Galtung, J. & Ruge, M. (1965) 'The Structure of Foreign News: The Presentation of the Congo, Cuba and Cyprus Crises in Four Newspapers', *Journal of International Peace Research 1*: 64–90.

Georgiou, M. & Silverstone, R. (2007) 'Diasporas and Contra-flows Beyond Nation-centrism', in Thussu, D.K., ed. *Media on the Move. Global Flow and Contra-flow.* London: Routledge, pp. 33–48.

Gerbner, G. & Marvanyi, G. (1977) 'The Many Worlds of the World's Press', *Journal of Communication 27*: 52–66.

Gerhards, J. & Schäfer, M.S. (2013) 'International Terrorism, Domestic Coverage? How Terrorist Attacks Are Presented in the News of CNN, Al Jazeera, the BBC, and ARD', *The International Communication Gazette* 76 (1): 3–26.

Gitlin, T. (1980) *The Whole World Is Watching.* Berkeley: University of California Press.

Golan, G. (2006) 'Inter-media Agenda Setting and Global News Coverage. Assessing the Influence of the *New York Times* on Three Network Television Evening News Programs', *Journalism Studies 7* (2): 323–333.

Golan, G. (2008) 'Where in the World Is Africa? Predicting Coverage of Africa by US Television Networks', *The International Communication Gazette 70* (1). 41–57.

Graddol, David. (1994) 'The visual accomplishment of factuality', in D. Graddol and O. Boyd-Barrett (eds), Media Texts: Authors and Readers. Clevedon: Multilingual Matters in association with the Open University, pp. 136-57.

Groothues, F. (2004) Television news and the European public sphere: A preliminary investigation. Centre for European Political Communications: European Political Communication Working Paper Series Issue 6/04.

Grosswiler, P. (2004) 'Continuing Media Controversies', in de Beer, A. & Merrill, J.C., eds., *Global Journalism. Topical Issues and Media Systems*. Boston: Pearson, pp. 112–127.

Grusin, R. (2010) *Premediation. Affect and Mediality after 9/11*. Houndmills: Palgrave Macmillan.

Gunaratne, S.A. (2007) 'A Systems View of "International" Communication, Its Scope and Limitations', *Global Media and Communication* 3: 267–271.

Gurevtich, M. & Kavoori, A.P. (1994) 'Global Texts, Narrativity and the Construction of Local and Global Meanings in Television News', *Journal of Narrative and Life History* 4 (1&2): 9–24.

Gutsche, R.E. (2014) 'News Place-making: Applying "Mental Mapping" to Explore the Journalistic Interpretive Community', *Visual Communication* 13 (4): 487–510.

Hachten, W.A. & Scotton, J.F. (2007) *The World News Prism*. Oxford: Wiley-Blackwell.

Hackett, R.A. & Zhao, Y. (eds.) *Democratizing Global Media: One World, Many Struggles*. Oxford: Rowman & Littlefield.

Hafez, K. (2007) *The Myth of Media Globalization*. Cambridge: Polity.

Hafez, K. (2011) 'Global Journalism for Global Governance? Theoretical Visions, Practical Constraints', *Journalism* 12 (4): 483–496.

Hagey, K. & Tau, B. (2011) 'Al-Jazeera has fans in Obama W.H.', Politico, 17 April, http://www.politico.com/news/stories/0411/53339.html.

Hahn, O. & Lönnendonker, J. (2009) 'Transatlantic Foreign Reporting and Foreign Correspondents After 9/11. Trends in Reporting Europe in the United States', *International Journal of Press/Politics* 14 (4): 497–515.

Hall, S. (1992) 'The West and the Rest: Discourse and Power', in Hall, S. & Gieben, B., eds. *Formations of Modernity*. Open University, pp. 275–331.

Hall, S., ed. (2007) *Representation: Cultural Representations and Signifying Practices*. London: Sage.

Hall, S., Critcher, C., Jefferson, J., Clarke, J. & Roberts, B. (1978) *Policing the Crisis*. London: Macmillan.

Hallin, D. (1986) 'Cartography, Community, and the Cold War', in Manoff, R.K. & Schudson, M., eds., *Reading the News*. New York: Pantheon Books.

Hallin, D. & Mancini, P. (2004) *Comparing Media Systems: Three Models of Media and Politics*. Cambridge: Cambridge University Press.

Halsall, R. (2006) 'Towards a Phenomenological Critique of Mediated Cosmopolitanism'. Paper presented at the annual meeting of the International Communication Association, Dresden, June 16th.

Hamelink, C. (2009) 'Internationalizing Media Ethics Studies', in Thussu, D.K., ed. *Internationalizing Media Studies*. London: Routledge, pp. 249–253.

Hamilton, J. M. & Jenner, E. (2004) 'Redefining Foreign Correspondence', *Journalism* 5 (3): 301–321.

Handley, R.L. & Rutigliano, L. (2012) 'Journalistic Field Wars: Defending and Attacking the National Narrative in a Diversifying Journalistic Field', *Media, Culture & Society 34* (6): 744–760.

Hanitzsch, T. et al. (2013) 'Interest in Foreign News', in Cohen, A.A., ed. *Foreign News on Television. Where in the World Is the Global Village?* New York: Peter Lang, pp. 171–190.

Hanitzsch, T. & C. Mellado (2011) 'What Shapes the News Around the World? How Journalists in Eighteen Countries Perceive Influences on Their Work', *International Journal of Press/ Politics 16* (3): 404–426.

Hanitzsch, T. & F. Hanusch (2012) 'Does Gender Determine Journalists' Professional Views? A Reassessment based on Cross-national Evidence', *European Journal of Communication 27* (3): 257–277.

Hannerz, U. (2000) *Foreign News: Exploring the World of Foreign Correspondents*. Chicago: The University of Chicago Press.

Hannerz, U. (2004) 'Cosmopolitanism', in Nugent, D. & Vincent, J. (eds) *A Companion to the Anthropology of Politics*. Oxford: Blackwell, pp. 69–85.

Hanusch, F. (2009) 'A Product of Their Culture. Using a Value Systems Approach to Understand the Work Practices of Journalists', *The International Communication Gazette 71* (7): 613–626.

Hanusch, F. (2014) 'The Geography of Travel Journalism: Mapping the Flow of Travel Stories about Foreign Countries', *The International Communication Gazette 76* (1): 47–66.

Heikkilä, H. (2007) 'Beyond "Insofar as" Questions. Contingent Social Imaginaries of the European Public Sphere', *European Journal of Communication 22* (4): 427–441.

Held, David (2002) "Cosmopolitanism: Ideas, Realities and Deficits", in David Held and Anthony McGrew, eds. *Governing Globalization. Power, Authority and Global Governance.* "Polity," chapter 15, pp. 305–323.

Held, D. (2004) 'Democratic Accountability and Political Effectiveness from a Cosmopolitan Perspective', *Government and Opposition* 39 (2): 364–391.

Hepp, A. & Couldry, N. (2009) 'What Should Comparative Media Research Be Comparing? Towards a Transcultural Approach to "Media Cultures"', in Thussu, D.K., ed. *Internationalizing Media Studies*. London: Routledge, pp. 32–47.

Herman, E. & McChesney, R. (2000) 'The Global Media' in Held, D. & McGrew, A. *The Global Transformations Reader*. Cambridge: Polity, pp. 216–229.

Hessel, S. (2011) *Time for Outrage (Indignez-Vous!)*. New York: Hachette.

Heyman, S. (2008) 'A Voice of Mother Russia, in English', *The New York Times*, May 18th.

Hjarvard, S. (2008) 'The Mediatization of Society. A Theory of the Media as Agents of Social and Cultural Change', *Nordicom Review* 29 (2): 105–134.

Holly, W. (2008) 'Tabloidisation of Political Communication in the Public Sphere', in Wodak, R. & Koller, V. (eds.) *Handbook of Communication in the Public Sphere*. Berlin: Moutin de Gruyter, pp. 317–341.

Hoover, S.M. (2011) 'Media and the Imagination of Religion in Contemporary Global Culture', *European Journal of Cultural Studies 14* (6): 610–625.

Hopper, P. (2007) *Understanding Cultural Globalization*. Cambridge: Polity.

Hoskins, A. & O'Loughlin, B. (2010) *War and Media. The Emergence of Diffused War*. Cambridge & Malden: Polity.

Huxley, A. ([1932]1994) *Brave New World*. London: Flamingo.

Ioffe, J. (2010) 'What Is Russia Today? A Kremlin Propaganda Outlet Has an Identity Crisis', *Columbia Journalism Review* September/October, http://www.cjr.org/feature/what_is_russia_today.php?page=all, accessed 9 October 2010.

Jones, J.P. & Baym, G. (2010) 'A Dialogue on Satire News and the Crisis of Truth in Postmodern Political Television', *Journal of Communication Inquiry 34* (3): 278–294.

Kaitatzi-Whitlock, S. (2011) 'The Political Economy of Political Ignorance', in Wasko, J., Murdock, G. & Sousa, H. (eds.) *The Handbook of Political Economy of Communications*. Oxford: Blackwell, pp. 458–481.

Kariel, H.G. & Rosenvall, L.A. (1983) 'Cultural Affinity Displayed in Canadian Daily Newspapers', Journalism Quarterly 60: 431–6.

Kaldor, M. (2003) *Global Civil Society. An Answer to War*. Cambridge: Polity.

Kavoori, A.P. (2007) 'Thinking Through Contra-flows: Perspectives from Post-colonial and Transnational Cultural Studies', in Thussu, D.K., ed. *Media on the Move. Global Flow and Contra-flow*. London: Routledge, pp. 49–64.

Keane, J. (2003) *Global Civil Society?* Cambridge: Cambridge University Press.

Kim, J., et al. (2007) 'The Influence of Geopolitics and Foreign Policy on the US and Canadian Media: An Analysis of Newspaper Coverage of Sudan's Darfur Conflict', International Journal of Press/Politics 12(3): 87–95.

Kim, K. & Barnett, G.A. (1996) 'The Determinants of International News Flow: A Network Analysis', *Communication Research 23*: 323–352.

Kiselev, D. (2014) 'Russia and the West Are Trading Places on Freedom of Speech', *The Guardian*, April 10th.

Kiser, E. (1996) 'The Revival of Narrative in Historical Sociology: What Rational Choice Theory Can Contribute', *Politics & Society 24*: 249–71.

Krotz, F. (2009) 'Mediatization: A Concept with Which to Grasp Media and Societal Change', in Lundby, K., ed. *Mediatization. Concept, Changes, Consequences*. New York: Peter Lang, pp. 21–40.

Kruckeberg, D. & Tsetsura, K. (2004) 'International Journalism Ethics', in de Beer, A. & Merrill, J.C., eds., *Global Journalism. Topical Issues and Media Systems*. Boston: Pearson, pp. 84–92.

Kupe, T. (2013) 'Globalization from My African Corner', *Media, Culture & Society* 35 (1): 139–146.

Kuppens, A. & Mast, J. (2012) 'Ticket to the Tribes: Culture Shock and the "Exotic" in Intercultural Reality Television', *Media, Culture & Society 34* (7): 799–814.

Labov, W. & Waletsky, J. (1967) 'Narrative Analysis: Oral Versions of Personal Experience', in Helm, J. (ed) *Essays on Verbal and Visual Arts*. Seattle: University of Washington Press.

Larsen, P. (2002) 'Mediated Fiction', in Jensen, K. B. (ed) *A Handbook of Media and Communications Research*. London: Routledge, pp. 117–37.

Lee, S. (2005) 'A Theoretical Model of National Image Processing and International Public Relations'. Paper presented at the annual meeting of the International Communication Association, New York, http://citation.allacademic.com/meta/p_mla_apa_research_citation/0/1/1/9/3/p11934_index.html (accessed 10 October 2015).

Lee, S. (2007) 'International Public Relations as a Predictor of Prominence of US News Coverage', Public Relations Review 33(2): 158–65.

Leung, L. (2009) 'Mediated Violence as "Global News": Co-opted "Performance" in the Framing of the WTO', *Media, Culture & Society 31* (2): 251–269.

Lieblich, A. et al. (1998) *Narrative Research: Reading, Analysis and Interpretation*. Thousand Oaks CA and London: Sage

Lindén, J. (2005) '"Media and telecom need to cooperate more". Interview on convergence with Johan Lindén from Sveriges Television', Eurescom mess@age, http://archive.eurescom.eu/message/messageOct2005/interview_with_Johan_Linden_from_SVT.asp, accessed 9 March 2011.

Linklater, A. (2012) 'The Global Civilizing Role of Cosmopolitanism', in Delanty, G., ed. *Routledge Handbook of Cosmopolitan Studies*. London: Routledge, pp. 60–71.

Lorenzo-Dus, N. and Bryan, A. (2011) "Recontextualizing Participatory Journalists' Mobile Media in British Television News: A Case Study of the Live Coverage and Commemorations of the 2005 London Bombings", *Discourse and Communication* 5 (1): 23–40

Louw, P.E. (2004) 'Journalists Reporting from Foreign Places', in de Beer, A. & Merrill, J.C., eds., *Global Journalism. Topical Issues and Media Systems*. Boston: Pearson, pp. 151–162.

Lull, J. (2007) *Culture-on-Demand: Communication in a Crisis World*. Oxford: Blackwell.

Lynch, M. (2006) *Voices of the New Arab Public: Iraq, Al-Jazeera and Middle East Politics Today*. New York: Columbia University Press.

Madianou, M. (2012) 'Humanitarian Campaigns in Social Media', *Journalism Studies 14* (2): 249–266.

Madikiza, L. & Bornman, E. (2007) 'International Communication: Shifting Paradigms, Theories and Foci of Interest', *Communicatio* 33 (2): 11–44.

Mahadeo, M. and McKinney, J. (2007) 'Media Representations of Africa: Still the Same Old Story?' *Voices From the Global South*, Issue 4/*Policy & Practice*, pp. 14–20.

Malek, A. & Kavoori, A.P. (1999) The Global Dynamics of News: Studies in International News Coverage and News Agendas. Stamford, CT: Ablex.

Manheim, J. & Albritton, R. (1984) 'Changing National Images: International Public Relations and Media Agenda Setting', *The American Political Science Review* 78 (3): 641–57.

Mano, W. (2009) 'Re-conceptualizing Media Studies in Africa', in Thussu, D.K., ed. *Internationalizing Media Studies*. London: Routledge, pp. 277–293.

Martell, L. (2010) *The Sociology of Globalization*. Cambridge: Polity.

Martinez, M. (2013) 'Once called "terror network," Al Jazeera America dares to enter U.S. cable market', http://edition.cnn.com/2013/01/04/world/al-jazeera/, accessed 5 January 2013.

Matheson, D. and Allan, S. (2009) *Digital War Reporting*. Cambridge and Malden: Polity.

Mattelart, T. (2009) 'Globalization Theories and Media Internationalization: A Critical Appraisal' in Thussu, D.K., ed. *Internationalizing Media Studies*. London: Routledge, pp. 48–60.

McCarthy, J. et al. (1996) 'Images of Protest', *American Sociological Review* 6 (3): 478–499.

McChesny, R.W. (2011) 'The Crisis of Journalism and the Internet', in Meikle, G. & Redden, G., eds., *News Online. Transformations and Continuities*. Houndmills: Palgrave Macmillan, pp. 53–68.

McChesney, R.W. (2013) *Digital Disconnect. How Capitalism Is Turning the Internet Against Democracy*. New York: The New Press.

McLuhan, M. & Gordon, W. T. (2013/1964) *Understanding Media. The Extensions of Man* (Critical Edition). Gingko Press.

McLuhan, M. (2008/1962) *The Gutenberg Galaxy*. Toronto: University of Toronto Press.

McMillin, D.C. (2007) *International Media Studies*. Oxford: Blackwell.

McPhail, T. (2014) *Global Communication. Theories, Stakeholders, and Trends*, 4th edition. Malden: Wiley Blackwell.

Meltzer, K. (2012) 'The US Launch of Al Jazeera English in Washington, DC: An Analysis of American Media Coverage', *Journalism 14*(5): 661–677.

Mendieta, E. (2012) 'Interspecies cosmopolitanism', in Delanty, G., ed. *Routledge Handbook of Cosmopolitan Studies*. London: Routledge, pp. 276–288.

Merrill, J.C. (2004a) 'Global Press Philosophies', in de Beer, A. & Merrill, J.C., eds., *Global Journalism. Topical Issues and Media Systems*. Boston: Pearson, pp. 3–18.

Merrill, J.C. (2004b) 'International Media Systems: An Overview', in de Beer, A. & Merrill, J.C., eds., *Global Journalism. Topical Issues and Media Systems*. Boston: Pearson, pp. 19–34.

Meskimmon, M. (2012) *Contemporary Art and the Cosmopolitan Imagination*. London: Routledge.

Meyrowitz, J. (1999) 'No Sense of Place: The Impact of Electronic Media on Social Behavior', in Mackay, H. & O'Sullivan, T., eds., *The Media Reader: Continuity and Transformation*. London: Open University/Sage.

Mignolo, W.D. (2012) 'De-colonial Cosmopolitanism and Dialogues Among Civilizations', in Delanty, G., ed. *Routledge Handbook of Cosmopolitan Studies*. London: Routledge, pp. 85–100.

Mihelj, S. (2007) 'The European and the National in Communication Research', *European Journal of Communication 22* (4): 443–459.

Miladi, N. (2006) 'Satellite TV News and the Arab Diaspora in Britain: Comparing Al-Jazeera, the BBC and CNN', *Journal of Ethnic and Migration Studies 32*(6): 947–960.

Miles, H. (2005) *Al-Jazeera: The Inside Story of the Arab News Channel That Is Challenging the West*. New York: Grove Press.

Morley, D. & Robins, K. (1995) *Spaces of Identity. Global Media, Electronic Landscapes and Cultural Boundaries*. London: Routledge.

Morris, N. & Waisbord, S. (2001) *Media and Globalization: Why the State Matters*. Lanham, MD: Rowman & Littlefield.

Mouffe, C. (2005) *On the Political*. London: Routledge.

Mowlana, H. (1997) *Global Information and World Communication: New Frontiers in International Relations*. London: Sage.

Moyo, L. (2010) 'The Global Citizen and the International Media. A Comparative Analysis of CNN and Xinhua's Coverage of the Tibetan Crisis', *The International Communication Gazette*, *72* (2): 191–207.

Mujica, C. & Hanitzsch, T. (2013) 'Gatekeepers on Decision-Making in Foreign News', in Cohen, A.A., ed. *Foreign News on Television. Where in the World Is the Global Village?* New York: Peter Lang, pp. 209–224.

Myers, G., Klak, T. & Koehl, T. (1996) 'The Inscription of Difference: News Coverage of the Conflicts in Rwanda and Bosnia', *Political Geography 15* (1): 21–46.

Nava, M. (2007) *Visceral Cosmopolitanism: Gender, Culture and the Normalisation of Difference*. Oxford & New York: Berg.

Norris, P. (1995) 'The Restless Searchlight: Network News Framing of the Post-Cold War World', *Political Communication 12*: 357–370.

Norris, P. & Inglehart, R. (2012) 'The Persistence of Cultural Diversity Despite Cosmopolitanism', in Delanty, G., ed. *Routledge Handbook of Cosmopolitan Studies*. London: Routledge, pp. 166–177.

Ogan, C., Willnat, L. Pennington, R. & Bashir, M. (2013) 'The Rise of Anti-Muslim Prejudice: Media and Islamophobia in Europe and the United States', *The International Communication Gazette' 76* (1): 27–46.

Ong, J.C. (2009) 'The Cosmopolitan Continuum: Locating Cosmopolitanism in Media and Cultural Studies', *Media, Culture & Society 31* (3): 449–466.

Orgad, S. (2008) '"Have You Seen Bloomberg?" Satellite News Channels as Agents of the New Visibility', *Global Media and Communication* 4 (3): 301–327.

Orgad, S. (2012) *Media Representation and the Global Imagination*. Cambridge: Polity.

Örnebring, H. & Rantanen, T. (2013) 'Editorial', *Global Media and Communication* 9 (3): 189–193.

Painter, J. (2008) *Counter-Hegemonic News. A Case Study of Al-Jazeera English and Telesur*. Oxford: Reuters Institute for the Study of Journalism.

Pantti, M. (2013) 'Getting Closer? Encounters of the National Media with Global Images', *Journalism Studies 14* (2): 201–218.

Papastergiadis, N. (2012) 'Aesthetic Cosmopolitanism', in Delanty, G., ed. *Routledge Handbook of Cosmopolitan Studies*. London: Routledge, pp. 220–232.

Papathanassopoulos, S. (2005) 'Europe: An Exemplary Landscape for Comprehending Globalisation', *Global Media and Communication 1* (1): 46–50.

Parameswaran, R. (2010) 'The Rise of China and India: Promising New Teaching and Research Directions for Global Media Studies', *Global Media and Communication* 6 (3): 285–290.

Paterson, C. (2008) 'Global Battlefields', in Boyd-Barrett, O. & Rantanen, T., eds. (1998) *The Globalization of News*. London: Sage, pp. 79–103.

Pensky, M. (2012) 'Cosmopolitan Memory', in Delanty, G., ed. *Routledge Handbook of Cosmopolitan Studies*. London: Routledge, pp. 254–266.

Peters, J.D. (1999) *Speaking into the Air*. Chicago: University of Chicago Press.

Peters, J.D. (2009) "Witnessing", in Paul Frosch and Amit Pinchchevsky, eds., *Media Witnessing. Testimony in the Age of Mass Communication*. Houndmills: Palgrave Macmillan, pp. 23–48.

Philo, G. (2004) 'The Problem of Ignorance: News Content and Audience', in Paterson, C.A. and Sreberny, A. (eds) *International News in the 21st Century*. Eastleigh: John Libbey Publishing.

Philo, G. and M. Berry (2004) *Bad News from Israel*. London: Pluto Press.

Pieterse, J.N. (2009) "Representing the Rise of the Rest as Threat. Media and Global Divides", *Global Media and Communication* 5 (2): 221–237.

Pieterse, J. N. (2004) *Globalization and Culture*. Lanham, MD: Rowman & Littlefield.

Pintak, Lawrence (2009) "Arab Media and the Al-Jazeera Effect", in Thomas L. McPhail, ed. *Global Communication. Theories, Stakeholders, and Trends*, 3rd edition. Malden and Oxford: Wiley-Blackwell, pp. 290–304.

Pollock, S., Bhaba, H., Breckenridge, C. & Chakrabarty, D. (2000) 'Cosmopolitanisms', *Public Culture 12* (3): 577–89.

Price, M. (2008) 'Governance, Globalism and Satellites', *Global Media and Communication 4* (3): 245–259.

Punathambekar, A. & Scannell, P. (2013) 'Back to the Future: Media and Communication Studies in the 21st Century', *Media, Culture & Society 35* (1): 3–8.

Rantanen, T. (2005) *The Media and Globalization*. London: Sage.

Rantanen, T. (2007) 'Flows and Contra-flows in Transitional Societies', in Thussu, D.K., ed. *Media on the Move. Global Flow and Contra-flow*. London: Routledge, pp. 165–181.

Reding, V. (2009) 'EU film support goes global', press release 9 January 2009, http://europa.eu/rapid/pressReleasesAction.do?reference=IP/09/26&format=HTML&aged=0&language=EN&guiLanguage=en, accessed 13 June 2009

Reese, S.D. (2008) 'Theorizing a Globalized Journalism', in Löffelholz, M. & Weaver, D., eds., *Global Journalism Research: Theories, Methods, Findings*. London: Blackwell, pp. 240–252.

Reporters Without Borders (2011a) "Wave of arrests of bloggers and activists", January 7th, http://en.rsf.org/spip.php?page=imprimir_articulo&id_article=39238.

Reporters Without Borders (2011b) "Internet censorship and attacks on journalists amid major street protests", January 26th, http://en.rsf.org/egypt-internet-censorship-and-attacks-on-26–01–2011,39400.html, accessed 31/01/11.

Reporters Without Borders (2011c) "Nawaat: Reporters Without Borders awards the 2011 Netizen Prize to Tunisian bloggers", March 11, http://en.rsf.org/nawaat-reporters-without-borders-11–03–2011,39776.html, accessed 11/03/11.

Resende, F. & Paes, A.B. (2011) 'The Arab Conflicts and the Media Discourse: A Brazilian Perspective', *Global Media and Communication 7* (3): 215–219.

Richardson, K. & Meinhof, U.M. (1999) *Worlds in Common? Television Discourse in a Changing Europe*. London: Routledge.

Riegert, K. (1998) "'Nationalising' Foreign Conflict: Foreign Policy Orientation as a Factor in Television News Reporting". Stockholm: University of Stockholm, Department of Political Science.

Robertson, A. (2000) 'Europa erzählt: Erzählanalyse und Fernsehnachrichten über Europa', in Deth, J. W. & König, T., eds., *Europäische Politikwissenschaft: Ein Blick in die Werkstatt*. Frankfurt: Campus.

Robertson, A. (2010) *Mediated Cosmopolitanism. The World of Television News*. Cambridge and Malden: Polity.

Robertson, A. (2012) 'Narrativanalys', in Boréus, K. & Bergström, G., eds., *Textens mening och makt*. Lund: Studentlitteratur, pp. 219–262.

Robertson, A. (2014) 'Euromedia: Integration and Cultural Diversity in a Changing Media Landscape', in McPhail, T., ed. *Global Communication*, 4th edition. Wiley-Blackwell.

Robertson, A. (2015) *Media and Politics in a Globalizing World*. Cambridge: Polity.

Robinson, P. (2002) *The CNN Effect*. London: Routledge.

Roche, M. (2012) 'Cosmopolitanism, Europe and Social Change: A Socio-historical Perspective on Cosmopolitan Order in Europe and the EU', in Delanty, G., ed. *Routledge Handbook of Cosmopolitan Studies*. London: Routledge, pp. 538–549.

Roselle, L., Miskimmon, A. & O'Loughlin, B. (2014) 'Strategic Narrative: A New Means to Understand Soft Power', *Media, War & Conflict* 7 (1): 70–84.

Rosenblum, M. (1993) *Who Stole the News? Why We Can't Keep up with What Happens in the World and What We Can Do About It*. New York: John Wiley & Sons.

Rosengren, K.E. (1974) 'International News: Methods, Data and Theory', *Journal of Peace Research 11*: 145–156.

Roudometof, V. (2005) 'Transnationalism, Cosmopolitanism and Glocalization', *Current Sociology*, 53 (1): 113–135.

Rowden, R. (1998–99) 'Developing Savages, Spreading Democracy: Popular Conceptions of North-South Relations', *Berkeley Journal of Sociology* 43: 149–187.

Rumford, C. (2012) 'Bordering and Connectivity: Cosmopolitan Opportunities', in Delanty, G., ed. *Routledge Handbook of Cosmopolitan Studies*. London: Routledge, pp. 245–253.

Sabry, T. (2009) 'Media and Cultural Studies in the Arab World: Making Bridges to Local Discourses of Modernity', in Thussu, D.K., ed. *Internationalizing Media Studies*. London: Routledge, pp. 196–213.

Saeed, O. (2014) 'Thank you for supporting #FREEAJSTAFF', Al Jazeera, http://blogs.aljazeera.com/blog/middle-east/thank-you-supporting-freeajstaff, accessed 2 October 2014.

Said, E. (1978/2003) *Orientalism*. London: Penguin.

Sakr, N. (2007) 'Challenger or Lackey? The Politics of News on Al-Jazeera', in Thussu, D.K., ed. *Media on the Move. Global Flow and Contra-flow*. London: Routledge, pp. 116–132.

Sakr, N. (2008) 'Diversity and Diaspora. Arab Communities and Satellite Communication in Europe', *Global Media and Communication* 4 (3): 277–300.

Salamandra, C. (2012) 'The Muhannad Effect: Media Panic, Melodrama, and the Arab Female Gaze', *Anthropological Quarterly* 85 (1): 45–78.

Scannell, Paddy (2004) "What Reality Has Misfortune?", *Media, Culture & Society* 26 (4): 573–584.

Schaefer, D.J. & Karan, K. (2010) 'Problematizing Chindia: Hybridity and Bollywoodization of Popular Indian Cinema in Global Film Flows', *Global Media and Communication* 6 (3): 309–316.

Schechter, D. (2013) 'Will Americans ever get to see Al Jazeera?'http://www.aljazeera.com/indepth/opinion/2013/01/2013149124977775.html, accessed 5 January 2013.

Schirato, T. & Webb, J. (2003) *Understanding Globalization*. London: Sage.

Scott, B. (2005) 'A Contemporary History of Digital Journalism', *Television and New Media* 6 (1): 89–126.

Scott, M. (2008) *Screening the World. How UK Broadcasters Portrayed the Wider World in 2007–8*. Research report commissioned by IBT, the Department for International Development, https://ueaeprints.uea.ac.uk/40650/.

Scott, M. (2009) 'Marginalized, Negative or Trivial? Coverage of Africa in the UK Press', *Media, Culture & Society 31* (4): 533–557.

Scott, M. (2014) *Media and Development. Development Matters*. London: Zed Books.

Segev, E. & Hills, T. (2013) 'When News and Memory Come Apart: A Cross-national Comparison of Countries' Mentions', *International Communication Gazette 76* (1): 67–85.

Seib, P. (2008) *The Al Jazeera Effect. How the New Global Media Are Reshaping World Politics*. Dulles: Potomac Books.

Seib, P., ed. (2012) *Al Jazeera English. Global News in a Changing World*. Palgrave Macmillan.

Shachar, N. (2014) 'Al-Jazeera trängs hårt av regionens ledare', *Dagens Nyheter*, 12 March, http://www.dn.se/nyheter/varlden/al-jazeera-trangs-hart-av-regionens-ledare/, accessed 12 March 2014.

Shafer, J. (2013) 'The new Medicis funding journalism', Reuters, 13 February, http://www.reuters.com/article/2014/02/13/shafer-medicis-idUSL2N0LI14K20140213, accessed 11 July 2014.

Shaw, I.S. (2012) 'Stereotypical Representations of Muslims and Islam Following the 7/7 London Terror Attacks: Implications for Intercultural Communication and Terrorism Prevention', *The International Communication Gazette 74* (6). 509–524.

Shaw, M. (2003) 'The Global Transformation of the Social Sciences', in Kaldor, M. et al. (eds.) *Global Civil Society 2003*. Oxford: Oxford University Press, pp. 35–44.

Shenker, J. (2013) 'Mediterranean migrant deaths: A litany of largely avoidable loss', The Guardian, 3 October, http://www.theguardian.com/world/2013/oct/03/mediterranean-migrant-deaths-avoidable-loss, accessed 3 October 2013.

Shoemaker, P.J. (1996) 'Hardwired for News: Using Biological and Cultural Evolution to Explain the Surveillance Function', Journal of Communication 46(3): 32–47.

Shohat, E. & Stam, R. (1994) *Unthinking Eurocentrism. Multiculturalism and the Media*. London: Routledge.

Shohat, E. and Stam, R. (2002) 'The Imperial Imaginary', in Askew, K. and Wilk, R.R., eds. *The Anthropology of Media. A Reader*. Oxford: Blackwell, pp. 117–147.

Shumow, M. (2012) 'Immigrant Journalism, Ideology and the Production of Transnational Media Spaces', *Media, Culture & Society 34* (7): 815–831.

Siapera, E. (2010) *Cultural Diversity and Global Media. The Mediation of Difference*. Chichester: Wiley-Blackwell.

Silverstone, R. (2007) *Media and Morality: On the Rise of the Mediapolis*. Cambridge: Polity.

Simmons, B.A. (2011) 'International Studies in the Global Information Age', *International Studies Quarterly* 55: 1–11.

Somers, M.R. (1994) 'The Narrative Constitution of Identity: A Relational and Network Approach', *Theory & Society* 23: 605–49.

Sorensen, J. (1991) 'Mass Media and Discourse on Famine in the Horn of Africa', *Discourse & Society* 2 (2): 223–242.

Sparks, C. (2007) 'What's Wrong with Globalization?' *Global Media and Communication* 3(2): 133–155.

Sparks, C. (2013) 'Global Media Studies: Its Development and Dilemmas', *Media, Culture & Society* 35 (1): 121–131.

Stepínska, A. et al. (2013) 'The Prevalence of News: Domestic, Foreign and Hybrid', in Cohen, A.A., ed. *Foreign News on Television. Where in the World Is the Global Village?* New York: Peter Lang, pp. 23–38.

Stevenson, N. (1999) *The Transformation of the Media. Globalisation, Morality and Ethics*. London: Longman.

Stevenson, N. (2003) *Cultural Citizenship: Cosmopolitan Questions*. Maidenhead: Open University Press.

Stevenson, R. L. (1992) 'Defining International Communication as a Field', *Journalism Quarterly* 69: 543–553.

Stråth, B., ed. (2000) *Europe and the Other and Europe as the Other*. Brussels: Peter Lang

Straubhar, J. (2008) *World Television: From Global to Local*. London: Sage.

Straubhar, J. (2010) 'Chindia in the Context of Emerging Cultural and Media Powers', *Global Media and Communication* 6 (3): 253–262.

Strydom, P. (2012) 'Modernity and Cosmopolitanism: From a Critical Social Theory Perspective', in Delanty, G., ed. *Routledge Handbook of Cosmopolitan Studies*. London: Routledge, pp. 25–37.

Szerszynski, B. & Urry, J. (2006) 'Visuality, Mobility and the Cosmopolitan: Inhabiting the World from Afar'. *Journal of Sociology* 57 (1): 113–131.

Szpunar, P.M. (2011) 'Western Journalism's "Other": The Legacy of the Cold War in the Comparative Study of Journalism', *Journalism* 13 (1): 3–20.

Tester, K. (1994) *Media, Culture and Morality*. London: Routledge.

Tharoor, Ishaan (2011) "Clinton Applauds Al Jazeera, Rolls Eyes at U.S. Media", *Time*, March 7th, http://globalspin.blogs.time.com/2011/03/03/clinton-applauds-al-jazeera-rolls-eyes-at-u-s-media

Thompson, J.B. (1995) The Media and Modernity. A Social Theory of the Media. Cambridge: Polity.

Thrall, A.T., Stecula, D. & Sweet, D. (2014) 'May We Have Your Attention Please? Human-Rights NGOs and the Problem of Global Communication', *The International Journal of Press/Politics* 19 (2): 135–159.

Thussu, D.K., ed. (2007) *Media on the Move. Global Flow and Contra-flow*. London: Routledge.

Thussu, D.K. (2009a) *News as Entertainment. The Rise of Global Infotainment*. London: Sage.

Thussu, D.K. (2009b) 'Why Internationalize Media Studies and How?' in Thussu, D.K., ed. *Internationalizing Media Studies*. London: Routledge, pp. 13–31.

Thussu, D.K. (2013) 'India in the International Media Sphere', *Media, Culture & Society 35* (1): 156–162.

Tjernström, V. (2008) 'Nordic Newspapers on the EU. European Political Journalism after "non" and "nee"', *Journalism* 9 (4): 516–536.

Tomlinson, J. (1999) *Globalization and Culture*. Cambridge: Polity.

Tomlinson, J. (2011) 'Beyond Connection: Cultural Cosmopolitan and Ubiquitous Media', *International Journal of Cultural Studies 14* (4): 347–361.

Tunstall, J. (1977) *The Media Are American: Anglo-American Media in the World*. London: Constable.

Udupa, S. (2012) 'Desire and Democratic Visibility: News Media's Twin Avatar in Urban India', *Media, Culture & Society 34* (7): 880–897.

UNESCO (1980) *Many Voices, One World. Towards a New, More Just and More Efficient Information and Communication Order*. Colchester: The Anchor Press.

Urry (2002) 'The Global Media and Cosmopolitanism', in Ostendort, B., ed. *Transnatl. Am.* Heidelberg: C. Winter, pp. 91–106.

Usher, Nikki (2011) "How Egypt's uprising is helping redefine the idea of a 'media event'", Nieman Journalism Lab, February 8th, http://www.niemanlab.org/2011/02/how-egypts-uprising-is-helping-redefine-the-idea-of-a-media-event/, accessed 11/02/09.

Varsamopoulou, E. (2009) 'The Idea of Europe and the Ideal of Cosmopolitanism in the World of Julia Kristeva', *Theory, Culture & Society* 26 (1): 24–44.

Vartanova, E. (2009) 'De-Sovietizing Russian Media Studies', in Thussu, D.K., ed. *Internationalizing Media Studies*. London: Routledge, pp. 214–227.

Van Ginneken, J. (1998) *Understanding Global News: A Critical Introduction*. London: Sage.

Van Leuven, S. & Joye, S. (2014) 'Civil Society Organizations at the Gates? A Gatekeeping Study of News Making Efforts by NGOs and Government Institutions', *The International Journal of Press/Politics 19* (2): 160–180.

Vernon, R. (2012) 'Cosmocitizens?' in Delanty, G., ed. *Routledge Handbook of Cosmopolitan Studies*. London: Routledge, pp. 316–325.

Vidmar-Horvat, K. (2010) 'Consuming European Identity. The Inconspicuous Side of Consumerism in the EU', *International Journal of Cultural Studies 13* (1): 25–41.

Virilio, P. (1989) *War and cinema: the logistics of perception*. London: Verso.

Virilio, P. (2007) *The Original Accident*. Cambridge: Polity.

Volkmer, I. (2003) 'The Global Network Society and the Global Public Sphere', *Development* 46 (2). 9–16.

Volkmer, I. (2005) 'News in the Global Public Space', in Allan, S. ed., *Journalism: Critical Issues*. Maidenhead: Open University Press, pp. 357–69.

von Pape, T. et al. (2013) 'Countries of Interest', in Cohen, A.A., ed. *Foreign News on Television. Where in the World Is the Global Village?* New York: Peter Lang, pp. 191–205.

von Twickel, N. (2010) 'Russia Today uses controversty to seek viewers', The St. Petersburg Times Issue 1557, 19 March, www.sptimes.ru/index.php?action_id=2&story_id=30993, accessed 16 February 2011.

Waisbord, S. (2013a) *Reinventing Professionalism. Journalism and News in Global Perspective*. Cambridge: Polity.

Waisbord, S. (2013b) 'Media Policies and the Blindspots of Media Globalization: Insights from Latin America', *Media, Culture & Society* 35 (1): 132–138.

Wallerstein, I. (1976) *The Modern World System*. New York: Academic Press.

Wallerstein, I. (1990) 'Culture as the Ideological Battleground of the Modern World-System', *Theory, Culture & Society* 7: 31–55.

Wasserman, H. (2011) 'Global Journalism Studies: Beyond Panoramas', *Communicatio* 37 (1): 100–117.

Weaver, D.H. (2004) 'Journalists: International Profiles', in de Beer, A. & Merrill, J.C., eds., *Global Journalism. Topical Issues and Media Systems*. Boston: Pearson, pp. 142–150.

Weaver, D.H. & Willnat, L. eds. (2012) The Global Journalist in the 21st Century. Abingdon: Routledge.

Wessler, H. et al. (2008) *Transnationalization of Public Spheres*. Houndmills: Palgrave.

Wessler, H. & Adolphsen, M. (2008) 'Contra-flow from the Arab World? How Arab Television Coverage of the 2003 Iraq War Was Used and Framed on Western International News Channels', *Media, Culture & Society* 30 (4): 439–461.

Wilhoit, G.C. & Weaver, D. (1983) 'Foreign News Coverage in Two U.S. Wire Services: An Update', *Journal of Communication* 33 (2): 132–148.

Wilke, J. et al. (2013) 'Countries of Location and Countries Involved', in Cohen, A.A., ed. *Foreign News on Television. Where in the World Is the Global Village?* New York: Peter Lang, pp. 63–85.

Wilke, J. & Heimprecht, C. (2013) 'Formal Features and Sources in Foreign News', in Cohen, A.A., ed. *Foreign News on Television. Where in the World Is the Global Village?* New York: Peter Lang, pp. 107–128.

Wilke, J., Heimprecht, C. & Cohen, A. (2012) 'The Geography of Foreign News on Television: A Comparative Study of 17 Countries', *The International Communication Gazette* 74 (4). 301–322.

Wilkinson, I. (2012) 'Humanitarianism and Cosmopolitanism', in Delanty, G., ed. *Routledge Handbook of Cosmopolitan Studies*. London: Routledge, pp. 400–413.

Williams, P. (2013) *Paul Gilroy*. London: Routledge.

Willnat, L. et al. (2013) 'Who Uses News, How Much, and Why?', in Cohen, A.A., ed. *Foreign News on Television. Where in the World Is the Global Village?* New York: Peter Lang, pp. 153–169.

Willnat, L. & Cohen, A.A. (2013) 'Self-Reflexivity of Gatekeepers on Content and Viewers of Foreign News', in Cohen, A.A., ed. *Foreign News on Television. Where in the World Is the Global Village?* New York: Peter Lang, pp. 225–249.

Willnat, L. & Martin, J. (2012) 'Foreign Correspondents-An Endangered Species?' in D.H. Weaver & L. Willnat, eds. The Global Journalist in the 21st Century. Abingdon: Routledge.

Winseck, D. & Jin, D.Y. (2011) *The Political Economies of Media. The Transformation of the Global Media Industries*. London: Bloomsbury.

Wojcieszak, M.E. (2007) 'Al Jazeera. A Challenge to Traditional Framing Research', *The International Communication Gazette* 69 (2): 115–128.

Wu, H.D. (2007) 'A Brave New World for International News? Exploring the Determinants of the Coverage of Foreign Nations on US Websites', *The International Communication Gazette* 69(6): 539–551.

Yegenoglu, M. (2012) 'Cosmopolitanism and Migrancy', in Delanty, G., ed. *Routledge Handbook of Cosmopolitan Studies*. London: Routledge, pp. 414–424.

Zayani, M., ed. (2005) *The Al Jazeera Phenomenon: Critical Perspectives on New Arab Media*. Boulder: Paradigm Publishers.

Zednik, R. (2002) 'Perspectives on War. Inside Al Jazeera', *Columbia Journalism Review*, Issue 2, March/April, www.cjr.org/issues/2002/2/war-zednik.asp, accessed 24 March 2006.

Zhao, Y. (2009) 'Rethinking Chinese Media Studies: History, Political Economy and Culture', in Thussu, D.K., ed. *Internationalizing Media Studies*. London: Routledge, pp. 175–195.

Zohry, K.A., ed. (2011) Al Jazeera 15: A Special Publication on Al Jazeera's 15th Anniversary. www.aljazeerastory.net.

INDEX

A

Abbas, W., 47, 48
activists and elites, 5, 57
Adams, P.C., 67, 81
Adolphsen, M., 23
Africa, 5, 6, 42, 105–7
age of imperialism, 5
Al Arabya, 121
Ali, A.H., 75
Al Jazeera effect, 24
Al Jazeera English (AJE), 11, 13–15, 17, 20, 23–26, 28–32, 35–36
  Arab uprisings and, 50–52
    referendum in Sudan and Palestine Papers and, 50–51
  code of ethics and, 29
  counter-hegemonic channel and, 26
  diversity and, 28, 31, 41
  global channel and, 113
  global gaze and, 42
  imprisonment of three journalists and, 34, 56
  narratives of justice and, 76
  prototype for the new breed of news organizations and, 25
  the South and, 42
  space of Europe and, 73–74
  statistics and, 14, 28
  winning the information war and, 24, 56
  See also Arab uprisings, counter hegemonic media, the gaze
Albritton, R., 25
American intervention, 77
Americanization, 19
Anglo-Saxon
  capital, 35
  channels, 42
  model of media and politics, 14
  monopoly, 28
  perspectives, 5, 111
anti-capitalist critique, 35

anti-immigration parties, 4, 63, 65
Appadurai, A., 86
Appiah, K.A., 82–83, 87
Arab uprisings, 37, 44, 45–52
authoritarian regimes and violent repression and, 45
Jasmine Revolution, the Arab Spring or the Arab Awakening and, 46, 58
Arendt, H., 65
architectural imagery, 105
Assange, J., 27
Atlas Reports, 37
Azran, T., 23

B

BBC/CNN approach, 23
BBC World (BBCW), 5, 13–15, 24, 29, 32, 33, 35–36
Arab uprisings and, 49–50, 57
British domestic political culture and, 33
organizational ethos and, 33
space of Europe and, 72–73
statistics and, 14
Voice of America and, 25
See also Arab uprisings
Bakhtin, M., 64
Baradai, 48
Barnett, G.A., 6, 18
Baudrillard, J., 117
Bauman, Z., 65
bearing witness, 52–57, 92–93, 106
Also see witnessing
Beck, U., 2, 87, 88, 89, 117, 118
being global is being local, 30, 31, 35, 58, 115
Benhabib, S., 120
Bennett, W.L., 11
Berger, G., 8–9, 23
Berglez, P., 9–10, 60, 72–73, 80, 110, 115–16, 120
Berry, M., 114
Bhabha, H., 68, 87
big business equals bad journalism, 21–22
Bimber, B., 11
Bjerström, E., 6
Blaagaard, B., 11
Bloomfield, S., 23
Boltanski, L., 52, 88
Boulding, K., 64, 119
Bourdieu, P., 19
Bowen, J., 59
Boyd-Barrett, O., 19
Bruegel, P. and the Elder's painting of the Tower of Babel, 2–3, 18, 21
Bruner, J., 88
Bryan, A., 53

C

CCTV, 20, 32
CNN International (CNNI), 5, 13–15, 24, 27, 29, 32, 35, 121
Arab uprisings and, 46–49
CNN Effect, 14
statistics and, 14
See also Arab uprisings
Caesar, J., 40
Castells, M. 12
Caquard, S., 68, 81, 85
Chadwick, A., 118
Chang, T-K., 7, 12, 18
change, 58
character-driven narratives and Everyman's eyes, 30
Chatman, S., 88
Cheah, P., 10
Chernilo, D., 65
Chouliaraki, L., 11, 38, 65, 88
Clancy, J. 48
Clausen, L., 8–9
Clinton, H., 24
Cohen, A.A., 7
collective solutions, 119
colliding worlds, 17–21

corporate interests and information rights and needs and, 17
different funding forms and different political systems and, 17
colonialism, 18, 19, 20
common theoretical understandings, 82
common thread, 65, 86–87
communication ecology, 15
communicative architecture, 8, 39, 112
communicative geography, 66, 116
comparative research, 63
conflict reporting, 23, 36, 38
connectivity, 58
consequences of government foreign policies, 33–34
constitution of crisis, 45
construction of a moral order, 10
consumer sovereignty, 19
consumption of first person narratives, 52
context of inquiry, 4–8
contra-flows, 22–26
corporate colonization, 20
See also colonialism
corporate profit incentives, 35
cosmopolitan, 3, 87, 110, 116
connection and, 116
conversations and, 83
geographies and, 68, 80–83
imagination and, 65
landscape and, 117
narratives and, 79, 86
optimism and, 39, 65
reading and, 82
theorists and, 62
See also narrative strategies
cosmopolitanism, 11, 36, 59, 61, 65, 69, 80, 81, 82, 88, 89, 109, 115–16
civic cosmopolitan and, 44
conflict and, 112
invisible cosmopolitans and, 23
mediated and, 61, 115
moral dimension and, 65, 86
new news media and, 11
relationships between the media and, 38
search for contrasts and, 65
Cottle, S., 5, 7–8, 10, 19, 23, 38, 39, 40, 41, 43, 52, 53, 58, 59, 60, 111, 112, 114, 115, 117
Couldry, N., 59, 65, 81
counter hegemonic media, 13, 22–26, 41, 42, 43, 45, 111, 112
crisis, 114–115
communication and, 40, 45
dissent and, 114
headlines and, 44
critical
political economy, 18, 20–21, 35
scholarly perspectives, 35, 38
theoretical perspectives and, 17–21
cultural globalization, 19
cultural imperialism, 19
cultural integration, 119
Czarniawska, B., 88

D

Daily Telegraph, 81
day of rage, 55
Delanty, G., 65, 86
Dencik, L., 5, 9, 33, 65, 111, 112
deregulation, 23
determinants of foreign news coverage, 6–7
deterritorialized Meyrowitzian world, 88–89
d'Haenens, L., 7
Dharwadker, V., 68, 80
diasporic communities, 23
difference, 4, 12, 29, 31, 35, 63, 82, 86, 87, 106, 112, 116, 119
channels and, 4, 121
representation and, 4, 120
Saussure and, 64, 82
Also see representation
digital/online activism, 46, 47, 51
discursive connections, 38, 49, 56, 58, 65, 66, 68, 87
Also see global discursive events
discursive map, 63
discursive power, 10, 59, 64, 67, 110
distribution of crisis headlines, 43

diversity, 4, 12, 21, 35, 57, 63, 81
dominant narratives of the market, 66, 117
Doucet, L., 55, 57, 58
dramaturgy of the media, 6, 58
Dyer, R., 64
Dzyadko, T., 23

E

East-West bifurcation in Cold War accounts of world politics, 42, 60, 112
The Economist, 5, 121
effects of truth, 52
Egyptian activists, 51
Electronic Colonialism Theory, 19, 117
el-Ibiary, R., 24
elites, 80
  See also activists and elites
el-Nawawy, M., 23
Eurodata, 11
Europe, 69–70
  respect and, 106–7
European South, 66, 85
European Union (EU), 4, 19

F

Facebook, 11, 28, 47, 48, 51
Facebook Revolution, 46
Fahmy, M., 59, 113
fascism, 4
fashion politics, 101
Figenschou, T.U., 14, 23, 57
Financial Times, 5
Fox News, 3, 32
France24, 20, 25
Freeman, B.C, 7, 25
Freemantle, J., 23, 27, 32
Freeview, 14
Frosh, P., 38, 52, 53, 87

G

Galtung, J, 6
the gaze, 63, 116
  cosmopolitan and, 89
  reversing the gaze and, 86, 112
  See also cosmopolitan
gender, 35, 54, 55, 57, 66
geo-linguistic constituences, 23
Georgiou, M., 23
Gerbner, G., 18
global, 8
  audience and, 4
  capitalism and, 18
  communication and, 3, 8, 19, 22, 64, 82
  communication flows and, 36
  culture and, 8, 121
  discursive events and, 10, 48
  economic crisis and, 11, 37
  imagination and, 116, 120
  interdependence and, 10
  market and, 22, 56
    trend towards regionalization, localization and heterogeneity and, 22
  media and, 38, 117
    911 and, 51
  media studies and, 5
  mediasphere and, 22
  networks and, 29, 110
  politics and, 25
    relationships and, 106
  public broadcaster and, 36
  public sphere and, 3, 52, 116–117
  south and, 63
  spaces and, 5, 10
  turn and, 6
  village and, 1–8
  See also space
global crises, 38, 39, 40–41, 58, 60, 66, 115, 117
  definition of, 40–41
  economics and, 45, 65, 115
  issue and frame and, 39

new wars and, 38, 40, 44
public definition and, 39
global journalists and journalism, 8–10, 25, 36, 60, 80, 115, 120
dispassionate reporting and, 67
issues are embedded in global processes and, 9
new breed of gatekeeper and, 25
purveyor of global infotainment and, 25
teachers, preachers, and ideologists and, 67
understanding why things matter and, 36
global order and imagination, 86
global television news, 1,8, 9, 11–13, 23, 25, 29, 35–36, 38–39, 62–63, 110, 117, 119, 120, 121
discourse and, 120
English-language broadcasts and, 13
impact and, 118
increasingly homogenous product and, 35
parallel universes and, 110
switcher between national and transnational communication and, 12
systematic comparison analysis and, 3, 32
universal values of professionalism and objectivity and, 13
globalization, 19, 59
Also see cultural globalization
globalization economies of post-colonial societies, 13
globalization of infotainment, 20, 38, 117
Google, 68
Google Earth, 51
Gorani, H., 14, 43, 47, 48, 111
Gordon, W.T., 2
Gosset, U., 25
Graddol, D., 89
Gramsci, A., 18
grander images of the world, 67
Greste, P., 59, 113
Grusin, R., 51, 114
The Guardian, 75
Gunaratne, S.A., 8
Gutsche, R.E., 68

H

Habermasian concerns, 3, 52
Hachten, W.A., 5, 121
Hafez, K., 9, 115
Hall, S., 1, 64, 65, 82
Hallin, D., 14, 66–67, 82, 89
Halsall, R., 10
Hannerz, U., 10, 62
hegemonic
market, 81
rationality, 65
theory, 18
hegemony of global news outlets, 17, 64
Herman, E., 19
Hessel, S., 59
Hetero-identification, 119
Heyman, S., 23
high helicopter views, 30, 79, 112
Hjarvardm S., 59
Holly, W., 19
homogenization or McDonaldization, 19, 22, 63, 81, 121
homogenous thesis, 41
Hong, Y., 7
Hopper, P., 19
Hoskins, A., 114
human rights abuses, 44
Huxley, A. and *Brave New World*, 62, 72, 81
hypermediacy of the web, 51

I

imagination, 86, 87, 88, 90, 92, 107, 110, 116
imagine the world as a whole, 10
immediacy of television monitoring, 51
information imbalances, 23
Instagram, 12
institutions of transnational communication, 4
instrumental dimensions, 58

interconnections between theoretical and empirical enquiry, 12
international
  communication, 8, 12
  news correspondence, 39
  politics, 25
  public relations, 25
Iraq conflict, 5
ireports, 48
Iskander, A., 23
Islamic State (IS), 59
ivory tower, 1–8, 13, 18, 61, 116, 117, 121
  metaphors and, 2–3
  the rise of the Rest and, 10

J

Jansson, A., 67, 81
Jones, A., 22
Joseph Kony's Lord's Resistance Army, 78
Journalism is not a crime, 34
Journalism Studies, 11
journalistic autonomy, 32
The Julian Assange Show, 27

K

Kaitztzi-Whitlock, S., 19
Kaldor, M., 38, 40
Kariel, H.G., 6
Kavoori, A.P., 8
Keane, J., 1
Kim, J., 7
Kim, K., 6, 18
King, L., 27
Kiselev, D., 23
Kiser, E., 88
Krotz, F., 59
Kupe, T., 23

L

Labov, W., 88
laissez-faire capitalism, 37
language theorists, 64
Larson, P., 88
Lee, H-M, 7
Lee, S., 7
Leung, L., 18
Lieblich, A., 88
Lorenzo-Dus, N., 53

M

mainstream media, 14
Malek, A., 8
Mancini, P., 14
Manheim, J., 25
mapping connectivity, 120
Martell, L., 19
Martin, J., 7
Marvanyi, G., 18
McChesney, R., 19, 21
McDonaldization or homogenization, 19, 22, 63, 81, 121
McLuhan, M., 2–3, 12
  global village and, 2, 119–21
  See also global village
McMillan, D.C., and research approaches, 5
McPhail, T., 18–19, 42, 117
media, 38, 46, 58, 111
  bias and, 21
  conglomerates and, 20
  connectivity and, 120
  discourse and, 20, 58, 106, 117
  ecology and, 24
  flows and, 5, 61, 63, 86, 112, 121
    corporations and, 21
    geography of, 24
  globalization and, 1, 13, 19, 22, 62, 116
    national autonomy and cultural diversity and, 19

logic and, 6
monopoly and, 21
narrative and, 63
ownership and, 20
representation and, 64
systems and, 19
technology and, 2, 24, 46, 57
metaphors and, 2
witnessing and, 42
politics of, 53
See also bearing witness, representation
mediapolis, 3, 10, 52, 110, 116, 119
mediascapes and landscapes, 2, 57, 61, 86, 114, 118, 121
mediated
crises, 39
interactions, 53, 59, 65
morality, 65
preconditions, 65
mediatization, 59
mega-conglomerates, 22
Mendieta, E., 65
Meskimmon, M., 10, 15
metaphorical frown, 65
middle-aged Englishman (MAE), 111
Mikhaleva, A., 26
Miladi, N., 23
Miskimmon, A., 7
Mladic, R., 75
mobile apps, 28
Mohamed, B., 59, 113
Morley, D., 10
Morsi, M., 113
Mowlana, H., 7
Mubarak's fall, 59
Murdoch, R., 21, 117, 118
Muslim Brotherhood, 113

N

narratives, 29, 54, 62, 63, 66, 80, 86, 87, 88, 91, 104, 105, 107, 115, 119, 120
African migrants in Europe and, 90, 91
counter narratives and, 85
Europe and, 105
function and, 119
hybridity and, 65, 87
imagination and, 82–83
maps and storytelling and, 65, 68, 81, 82
meta-narrative and, 57, 58
morally suppressive force of, 65
resistance and, 57
rhetorical and, 81
strategic and, 7, 81, 112–113
See also dominant narratives of the market
narrative structures and communicative frames, 7–8, 59, 69, 86, 104, 111–112
newsroom narrative or myth and, 8, 26, 65, 116
See also media narrative
nation branding, 7
national autonomy, 117
national narratives in the West, 10, 86
neo-liberal imperialism, 20
neo-liberal market solutions, 23
neo-Nazism, 4
new Medicis, 25
new warfare, 40
New World Information and Communication Order, 23
news from nowhere, 36
Newsweek, 5, 121
Nikolov, A., 26–28, 32, 112
notion of worlds, 8

O

Observer, 81
O'Laughlin, B., 7, 15, 114
oligopoly, 19, 117
Ong, J.C., 65, 86–87
Orgad, S., 10, 65, 66, 81
Orientalism, 85–86
the Other, 3, 62, 63, 64–65, 82, 86, 87, 89, 105, 107, 113, 116

distant and, 4, 65
five types and, 106
news channel and, 3
imaginative strategies and, 65
negative other and, 109
scholarly paradigms and, 3
moral space and, 11
othering, 12, 62, 64, 76, 86, 89, 91, 106, 107, 116, 118, 120
Africans and, 107
contemporary media artefacts and, 91
RT and, 81
UK and, 75
otherness, 64, 69, 81

P

Paes, A.B., 63
Painter, J., 23
Papastergiadis, N., 65
Parsons, N., 25, 115
periphery of the world system, 18
perspective-taking, 89, 107
Peters, J.D., 52, 87
Philo, G., 6, 114
Pieterse, J.N., 5, 10, 86
Pinchevsky, A., 38, 52, 53, 87
Pintak, L., 24
place, 67
deeply layered subjective experience and, 68
socially constructed and, 68
podcast, 28, 87
political change, 59
political communication and personalization strategies, 120
political-economic perspectives, 39, 117, 118
postcolonial scholarship, 62
Powers, S., 23
Priestley, J.B. and *We Live in Two Worlds*, 109–10
processes of political communication, 52
protesters in Khartoum, 49
proximity-related determinants, 6–7, 82
degree of proximity and, 65
See also determinants of foreign news coverage
Pullman, P. and *His Dark Materials*, 110
Putin, V., 27, 45

Q

R

Rai, M., 5, 7–8, 19, 23, 39, 52, 53, 58, 111, 112
Rand, A., 37–38
Atlas Shrugged and, 37–38, 109
philosophy of objectivism and, 37
Rantanen, T., 19
Rayner, B., 24
Reding, V., 19
rehabilitation, 78–79
narrative of Dennis, 78–79, 80, 81, 82, 116
representation, 4, 5, 63, 64–66, 88, 107, 116, 119
cultural sites and, 68
issues of, 12
mediality and, 114
Resende, F., 63
reversing the flow, 36, 81, 86
rich media produce poor democracy, 19
Riegert, K., 7
Robertson, A., 5, 8, 11, 19, 26, 64, 69, 88, 120
Robins, K., 10
Rodeo rehab and the Angolan Prison Rodeo, 79–80
Roselle, L., 7, 15, 50, 112
Rosenblum, M., 6, 25, 42, 120
Rosengren, K.E., 6
Rosenvall, L.A., 6

Rowden, R., 18
Ruge, M., 6
Russia Today (RT), 3, 13–15, 17, 20, 21–25, 26–28, 29, 32, 35–36
- Arab uprisings and, 50
- critiques of power and media and, 35
- discourse and, 60, 81
- diversity and, 27
- Driven to Edge and, 74
- injustice and, 76
- Kremlin and, 15, 26, 27, 32
- Money vs Medicine and, 74
- narrative and, 35
- Paranoid Android and, 75
- Pew Research Institute and, 27
- slogan and http://rt.com, 35
- space of Europe, 74–78
- suicide and austerity policies and, 76
- Syrian conflict and, 23
- Take-in Trauma and, 74
- Ukrainian crisis and, 23
- Wasted lives, 76–78
- *See also* Arab uprisings

Russian Federal Agency on Press and Mass Communications, 14

S

Saeed, O., 34
Said, E., 85, 86, 119
Sakr, N., 24, 35
Scannell, P., 52
Scotton, J.F., 5, 121
Segerberg, A., 11
Seib, P., 14, 23, 24, 25
Shafer, J., 25
Shakespeare and *The Tempest*, 62, 82
shared media culture, 19
Shaw, I.S., 10
Shoemaker, P.J., 7
Shohat, E., 10
Siapera, E., 10
Silverstone, R., 3, 10–11, 23, 52, 65, 110, 116, 119, 121
Simonyan, M., 26, 27
Sky News, 33
SMS alerts, 28
social media, 11, 38, 45–52, 58, 114
- connectivity and, 51
- contemporary mediations of crisis and, 11
- crowdsourced stills or video sequences and, 46, 53, 56
- force for change and, 49
- role in Arab uprisings and, 49
- understandings of politics and, 11
- *See also* Arab uprisings

soft power, 24–25, 81, 112, 118
Somers, M.R., 88
sophisticated images, 120
Southwell, B., 7
space, 62, 66–69, 76, 79, 81, 88, 116
- communicative and, 3, 87
- cosmopolitan and, 63
- cultural and political and, 5, 116
- Europe and, 69–76, 81
- liminal and, 79, 85
- margins of, 63, 80, 87
- mediated and, 119
- public and, 121
- shared and, 64, 65, 87, 110
- structured systems of connectivity and, 67
- *Also see* third space

spatial and temporal extension, 53
spectatorship, 52, 53
Speilberg's *Poltergeist*, 110
Stam, R., 10
stereotyping, 12, 36, 63, 64, 66, 81, 116
Stevenson, N., 3, 5, 10, 12, 65, 86
strategic locations, 85
strategic narratives, 7, 50
structural and communicative disparities, 18
Strydom, P., 65
Surprising Europe, 86, 90–107, 118
- *The Good Life* and, 102
- *Home Sweet Home* and, 90
- K-Nel and, 91–107
- loneliness versus community and, 105
- *Running Out of Luck* and, 99

Ssuuna Galooba and, 90–104
naturalism and, 91
Taking the Leap and, 90, 91
tales of destitution and, 97
themes of humans being treated like animals, 95, 99
symbolic conflict, 24
Syria, 59
systems of classification, 64

T

Tahir Square, 51–52, 59
See also Egyptian activists
tale of two Europes, 72
Taliban, 4
talking heads, 20, 47, 49, 104, 111
technologies and discourses, 10
Telesur, 20, 23
television, 11–12
See also global television news
television journalism and imagery and narrative techniques, 12
See also global journalism
testimony and sources of, 54
disrupted and, 55
Thani family of Qatar, 14, 25
non-profit journalism and, 25
theoretical perspectives, 65
third space, 68, 83, 85, 87
Thompson, J.B., 59
Thussu, D.K., 20, 22–23, 42, 117
Media on the Move and, 22–23
News as Entertainment and, 20, 22
Time, 5, 121
The Times, 81
Tomlinson, J., 3, 10, 109, 120
transborder flows, 12
transformation of codifications of Self and Other, 86
See also the Other
transformation of the media and our shared world, 5
transformative work of the global imagination, 119
transnational communicative space, 8, 23, 116
trials of cultural integration, 4
Tunstall, J., 36
Twitter, 11–12, 28, 47, 48, 51–52
hashtag Egypt, 48
internet blockade and, 48, 50

U

Udupa, S., 12–13
UK Office of Communications (ofcom), 29, 32
United Nations Educational, Scientific and Cultural Organization (UNESCO), 19
McBride Report and, 23
Urry, 10
Usher, N., 28

V

valorization of cultural diversity, 35
Van Ginneken, J., 20
van Gogh, T., 75
Verelst, C., 7
Vernon, R., 65
Verstehen, 120
Virilio, P., 24
voice of the voiceless, 32, 57, 66, 80, 112
von Twickel, N., 23

W

Waisbord, S., 13
Waletsky, J., 88
Wallerstein, I., 18–19
Wasserman, H., 8, 13, 15
Weaver, D.H., 8, 18
Wessler, H., 8, 23

the West and the Rest, 1, 41, 66, 107
rise of the rest and, 86
Western-global and the non-Western-national, 22
Western hegemony, 22, 35
Western media and amnesia, 34
where is Hosni Mubarak game, 48
Wilhoit, G.C., 18
Willnat, L., 7, 8
witnessing, 52–58, 87
choir of witnesses, 53
first-order and, 58
media and, 87
world of protest and, 53
Wojcieszak, M.E., 23
World Economic Forum, 30
World News Prism, 4, 121
world system theory, 18
World Vision Rehabilitation Centre, 78
worlds in collision, 34
worlds of global television news, 1
See also global television news
Wu, H.D., 6

X

Y

Youtube, 11, 14–15, 27, 28, 46, 51, 87

Z

Zednik, R., 23

GLOBAL CRISES AND THE MEDIA

Simon Cottle, *General Editor*

From climate change to the war on terror, financial meltdowns to forced migrations, pandemics to world poverty, and humanitarian disasters to the denial of human rights, these and other crises represent the dark side of our globalized planet. They are endemic to the contemporary global world and so too are they highly dependent on the world's media.

Each of the specially commissioned books in the *Global Crises and the Media* series examines the media's role, representation, and responsibility in covering major global crises. They show how the media can enter into their constitution, enacting them on the public stage and thereby helping to shape their future trajectory around the world. Each book provides a sophisticated and empirically engaged understanding of the topic in order to invigorate the wider academic study and public debate about the most pressing and historically unprecedented global crises of our time.

For further information about the series and submitting manuscripts, please contact:

Dr. Simon Cottle
Cardiff School of Journalism
Cardiff University, Room 1.28
The Bute Building, King Edward VII Ave.
Cardiff CF10 3NB
United Kingdom
CottleS@cardiff.ac.uk